D0916319

Frontispiece to Chandos Herald's *Life of Edward Prince of Wales and Aquitaine*, c.1385, showing the prince worshipping the Trinity, flanked by his motto (*Ich dene*) and feathers. (University of London MS. 1, f.1v)

# The Life
# and Campaigns of
# the Black Prince

from contemporary letters, diaries and chronicles,
including Chandos Herald's *Life of the Black Prince*

EDITED AND TRANSLATED BY
RICHARD BARBER

THE BOYDELL PRESS

First published 1979

Reprinted with new illustrations 1986
by The Boydell Press

First published in paperback 1997
Reprinted in paperback 2002

ISBN 0 85115 469 7

The Boydell Press is an imprint of Boydell & Brewer Ltd
PO Box 9, Woodbridge, Suffolk IP12 3DF, UK
and of Boydell & Brewer Inc.
PO Box 41026, Rochester, NY 14604–4126, USA
website: www.boydell.co.uk

A catalogue record for this series is available
from the British Library

Library of Congress Catalog Card Number: 97–23498

Printed in Great Britain by
St Edmundsbury Press Ltd, Bury St Edmunds, Suffolk

# Contents

# Illustrations

Frontispiece to Chandos Herald's *Life of Edward Prince of Wales and Aquitaine,* c. 1385, showing the prince worshipping the Trinity. (University of London MS. 1, f.3v)

1. Lead badge showing the prince adoring the Trinity, within the Garter, c. 1350-1376. (Trustees of the British Museum)

2. Edward III grants his son the principality of Aquitaine. From a contemporary copy of the original deed. (British Library MS Cotton Nero D.vi, 31)

3. Original deed granting the principality of Aquitaine to Edward Prince of Wales. (Public Record Office E30/1105)

4. John II, a fourteenth-century portrait now in the Louvre. (Photo Giraudon, Paris)

5. Effigy of the Black Prince in Canterbury cathedral. (National Monuments Record)

6. Pedro the Cruel: the contemporary funeral effigy now in the Museo Arquélogico Nacional, Madrid.

7. The painting of the Trinity on the tester above the prince's tomb in Canterbury cathedral: a reconstruction drawn by Professor E. W. Tristram. (Courtauld Institute of Art)

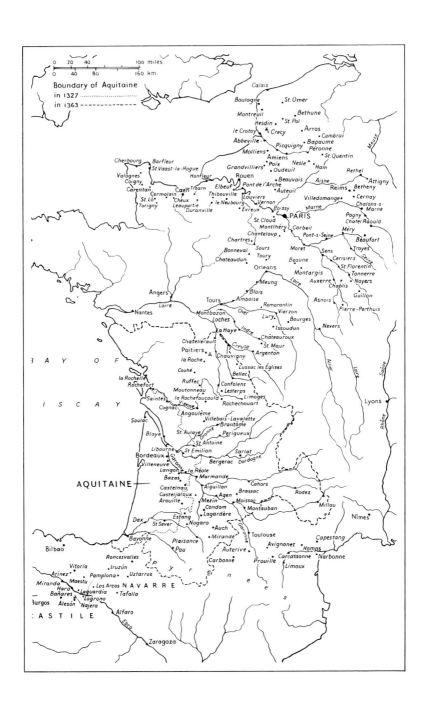

# Introduction

Edward of Woodstock, eldest son of Edward III, known since Tudor times as the Black Prince, is one of those heroes of traditional history books so impressive in his achievements as to seem slightly unreal. At sixteen he played the leading part in the fighting at Crécy; at twenty-six he captured the king of France at Poitiers; and eleven years later he restored Pedro of Castile to his throne at the battle of Najera. His exploits were chronicled by one of the most vivid writers of the Middle Ages, Jean Froissart; and it is Froissart's stories that have become part of our national legend.

Froissart was writing three or four decades after the events he described, and with the avowed purpose 'that the honourable enterprises, noble adventures, and deeds of arms, performed in the wars between England and France, may be properly related, and held in perpetual remembrance'. His materials were a large collection of earlier chronicles, mostly Flemish in origin, and oral accounts from the participants. The result is marvellous writing, sometimes very accurate, sometimes pure invention, sometimes 'gossip raised to the height of genius'. His picture is a fascinating portrait of fourteenth-century chivalry as it wanted to see itself.

There are, however, sources much closer to the events, and it is on these that the present volume draws. Most immediate are the reports sent home by the prince's companions-in-arms on the various campaigns, and the prince's own letters. At worst, they are sometimes mere lists of places; at best they give a clear idea of the hardships and difficulties of campaigning, its dangers and sheer fatigue. These are followed by slightly more elaborate campaign diaries: that for the Crécy campaign is incomplete, as the only manuscript breaks off a few days before the battle. For the battle of Crécy, the campaign leading up to Poitiers and for other exploits of the prince's, we have Geoffrey le Baker's chronicle, written about 1358–60, and using very similar sources. His account of the 1355 campaign is certainly based on a detailed campaign diary. Finally, there is the chronicle of Chandos Herald, a later verse composition,

7

which shows the prince as he appeared to an English writer in the 1380s. The author was herald to Sir John Chandos, the prince's companion in arms, and went with him on the Spanish campaign of 1367; his eyewitness account suffers from being put into rhyme, but is nonetheless most valuable. Each of the various sources is discussed at greater length in the introduction to the extracts.

### The prince's life

Despite the title usually given to Chandos Herald's poem, there is no really clear contemporary biography of him, because biography as a form was a Renaissance invention. So a brief outline of the prince's career is a necessary introduction to what follows.

Edward was born at Woodstock in June 1330, the eldest child of Edward III and his Flemish-born queen, Philippa of Hainault. He was given the usual knightly education of his contemporaries, and his interests seem to have been entirely in the direction of chivalry: among all his extravagant purchases of jewels, armour and clothes, there is never an indication of the intellectual interests of his son, Richard II. At the age of eight he was left as nominal regent when his father sailed for the Netherlands on the first campaign of the Hundred Years' War, the prolonged quarrel over the succession to the French throne which was to determine the course of Edward's life. Two years later in 1340, he watched his father sail once more, from Harwich, to meet a French fleet known to be cruising off Flanders in order to intercept him. The prince's messengers scoured the coast anxiously for news until word at last came of the first great English triumph over the French, at the battle of Sluys, where the French naval power was for a time destroyed. In 1345 he accompanied his father on a planned campaign to Flanders, which was cut short by the assassination of the pro-English van Artevelde, leader of the Flemish citizens. The following year saw his first battle honours, in the Crécy campaign, described below.

The Crécy campaign ended with the siege and capture of Calais, which was to be the English base in northern France for the next two hundred years. Geoffrey le Baker tells the story of how it was nearly lost only three years after its capture; but thanks to the personal efforts of the king and prince a French plot was foiled. The chief event of the years of peace after the taking of Calais was the creation of the Order of the Garter in 1348, whose founder-members were the prince's close companions; several distinguished commanders of an earlier generation were not included, while younger, less-known knights belonged to it, implying that it was based largely on ties of friendship rather than reward for service. A brilliant series of tournaments also took place about this time, in which the prince now took part, having been a mere spectator in earlier years. These were accompanied by lavish displays of wealth – magnificent costumes and armour, gifts of armour to companions, presents of gold to minstrels. There was another side to these scenes of youthful exuberance: the prince was also taking an increasing share in the administration of his estates, as one of the great landowners of the kingdom, travelling on occasions to Cornwall and Cheshire.

In the summer of 1350, another naval victory was won by the English, this time over the Spanish allies of the French, off Winchelsea. It was an isolated episode, however, because it was not renewed until 1355. A double campaign in Gascony and Northern France was planned, but in the event only the Gascon operations were carried out. In response to an appeal from the lords of Gascony, who had remained loyal to their English overlord since the beginning of the hostilities in 1338, the prince was sent out as leader of the expedition. His campaign in 1355 was a raid deep into enemy territory, designed for propaganda and economic reasons rather than to meet specific military objectives. His steward's report on the campaign emphasises the revenue lost to the French king by the destruction of such towns as Carcassonne, and the prince's army penetrated into areas which were believed to be completely safe from such incursions. After a winter spent in border warfare, the plan of 1355 was put into effect once more, and the prince marched northwards to join forces with the duke of Lancaster or his father. His father failed to cross the channel, and he was prevented from joining Lancaster by the breaking of the bridges over the Loire. Instead, he was forced to turn south, pursued by king John, 'the French usurper', whom he defeated against all odds at Poitiers. The campaign ended triumphantly as he returned to Bordeaux with the French king as his prisoner.

From 1356 to 1360, the action moved from the military to the diplomatic front. In October 1360 the treaty of Brétigny, intended as a definite settlement of the Anglo-French quarrel, was signed, and king John was released. Three years later, in July 1363, the prince sailed again for Gascony, to become lord of Aquitaine. He took with him Joan of Kent, whom he had married in 1361, an unexpected match which does not seem to have pleased his father. She was a great heiress, whose earlier marital career had involved a suit in the papal court between two lords claiming to be her rightful husband. Reputedly the greatest beauty of the age, she and the prince delighted in luxury for which his court at Bordeaux became a byword: on the birth of their eldest son, feasts and jousting of unparalleled splendour were held at Angoulême. But the political aspects of the prince's government were less brilliant: the Gascon lords who had at first welcomed him objected to his introduction of English attitudes towards government, centralised, efficient and hostile to their beloved local customs. There were rumblings of discontent within a year or two of his arrival; but such minor troubles were set aside in the autumn of 1366, when Pedro of Castile, an ally of the prince's father, demanded the prince's help in regaining his throne, which he had lost to his half-brother, Enrique of Trastamare. The prince's advisers seem to have been reluctant to offer him aid, but the prince was eventually able to persuade his father to allow him to go to Spain. The prince himself clearly saw the expedition as a welcome change from Gascon politics. In military terms it was a success, because Enrique ignored his French advisers and met the prince on the battlefield at Najera; but it was disastrous to the prince's health and finances. Forced to wait for payment by Pedro, who was totally unable to raise the vast sums he had promised, the prince caught some kind of dysentery which was to recur more and more violently for the rest of his life. He returned home to face discontent from both his unpaid army and from the Gascons whom he hoped to tax in order to meet his debts. The situation was cleverly exploited by Charles V, who had succeeded his father in 1364, and the disaffection of the Gascon lords became open revolt in 1369–70. The clauses of the treaty of Brétigny had never been fully carried out, and the French king therefore retained certain sovereign rights in Gascony, which were made the basis for a diplomatic campaign aimed at weaning the Gascons from their English allegiance. The prince rose from his sick-bed briefly in 1370 to take the city of

# Introduction

Limoges, which had rebelled against him even though its lord, the bishop, was godfather to the prince's son. But this last success (which was marked only by the destruction of the city and not by a massacre of the inhabitants) was brief. By the end of the year, it was plain that the prince could not continue to govern in Aquitaine, and he sailed for England early in 1371, shortly after the death of his eldest son.

His father was also now an invalid, and in the intervals between the attacks of his malady, the prince played some part in the government of England. A last attempt at a renewed French campaign in September 1372 was prevented by contrary winds after the army had embarked. In the spring of 1376, during the so-called 'Good Parliament', in which the abuses of a slack and corrupt government were attacked, possibly with the prince's support, his illness became acute, and he died at Westminster on 8 June. He was buried at Canterbury at the end of September.

Such, in bare outline, was the prince's career. What follows is an attempt to fill out the details of his moments of glory, using some remarkable documents which have hitherto been unknown to all except professional historians.

RICHARD BARBER

Note to 1997 reprint

I am most grateful to Dr Clifford Rogers for a number of comments and corrections based on his own forthcoming work *War Cruel and Sharp: English Strategy under Edward II, 1327–1360*, which have considerably improved my text.

# 1. Campaign letters: the Crécy campaign (1346)

## i. Introduction

The campaign of 1346 was originally intended to be an expedition to Gascony, but when the fleet was assembled, contrary winds prevented them from sailing for Bordeaux. Probably on the advice of Godfrey d'Harcourt, a Norman lord who had been in exile at the English court since the previous year, Edward III decided to attack Normandy instead. The raid was outstandingly successful: Caen was taken by assault, the French army was twice outmanoeuvred at the crossing of the Seine and the Somme. But for all the propaganda value of such an attack, which brought the English army to the walls of Paris itself, Edward and his men were the pursued, not the pursuers, when they made their spectacular fording of the Somme near Abbeville, and they started the battle of Crécy at a great disadvantage. Little of this emerges in the letters. They were written primarily as propaganda for home consumption; even after the English victory at Sluys in 1340, there was still considerable opposition to the war with France and the heavy taxation which resulted, and Edward and his commanders were anxious to paint a glowing picture of their achievements.

Nonetheless, the reports are immediate and direct, even if they do make light of some of the difficulties. The letters were usually written by secretaries, and even when the king or some other magnate signs them, the composition was probably left to men such as Richard Wynkeley, Michael Northburgh, and the chancellor of St Paul's, members of his clerical staff. Bartholomew Burghersh was the prince's 'tutor-in-arms', responsible for his knightly education, while the archbishop of Canterbury was head of the caretaker government in England during the king's absence.

## ii. Bartholomew Burghersh to John Stratford, archbishop of Canterbury, 17 July. (French)

Right reverend father in God and my most honoured lord, because I know that you would be very glad to have news of my lord the king and the fleet, I am writing to inform you that, when he had reviewed and provisioned all the ships for a fortnight, intending to go to Gascony, he set out in that direction, intending to pass the Needles at the end of the Isle of Wight and then to have sailed straight down Channel. But the wind was so adverse that he could not hold to this course at all, even though he lay at anchor a long time, to see if God would give him fair weather for a crossing. Since it did not please God that he should go in that direction, he decided to land wherever God should give him grace to do so, and thus arrived well and in good heart with all the fleet in the part of Normandy called the Cotentin on Wednesday before St Margaret's day, that is 12 July. On arrival my lord the prince was knighted, as well as Montagu, Mortimer, Roos and very many others. The town of Barfleur has been taken. My lord Warwick skirmished with the enemy, and won the day honourably; and my lord John Beauchamp and many other knights and squires engaged the enemy in raids and otherwise, and such enterprises have gone on the whole time. But the men at arms of the region have withdrawn into the castles and fortified towns, and the common people of the country have all come over to the king's side. That is all the news for the moment, my lord, except that the king and his army are setting out into the country to establish his rights by conquest, as God shall give him grace. Written at La Hogue, 17 July.

## iii. The chancellor of St Paul's to his friends in London, 17 July. (Latin)

This is to let you know that on 12 July we landed safely at a port in Normandy called La Hogue, near Barfleur. The king and many men at arms at once landed; and he immediately knighted his son the prince, Sir Roger Mortimer, Sir William Montagu and many others. And the prince himself knighted many others afterwards. On a number of occasions our handful of men defeated large numbers of the enemy, killing many, capturing more, and taking great enough booty each day, as they continue to do. There is no-one left in the surrounding countryside for twenty miles around who is offering resistance. We stayed in the place where we landed until the following Monday, St Kenelm's day. On that day it was decided that the next day we would set out towards the larger towns in Normandy and thus make our way into France, the Lord being our guide. Written at La Hogue, St Kenelm's day.

# iv. Michael Northburgh, 27 July. (French)

The king and his troops landed at St Vaast La Hogue on 12 July. He stayed there, to disembark the horses, to rest himself and his men and to bake bread, until the following Tuesday. He found eleven ships at La Hogue, eight of which had castles fore and aft; they were all burnt. On Friday, while the king was waiting, some of his men went to Barfleur, expecting to find people there, but found no-one to speak of. They found nine ships with castles fore and aft, two good fishing boats and other smaller boats, all of which were also burnt. The town was as good and large as Sandwich. After the men had left, the sailors burnt the town. Several good towns and manors in the surrounding countryside were burnt. On the Tuesday, when the king set out, he went to Valognes, where he stayed the night, and found adequate supplies. The next day he made a long march to the bridge over the Douve, which the men from Carentan broke down. The king had it repaired the same night, and crossed the next day to Carentan, which is only about a mile from the bridge. Carentan is as large as Leicester; a lot of wine and food was found there, and much of the town was burnt, the king being unable to prevent it. On the Friday, the king went and encamped in the villages in the country, near a river which was difficult to cross. The men of St Lô broke down the bridge, but the king had it repaired, and crossed the next day with his army: he encamped near the town. The townsmen had started to strengthen the place, and to gather men at arms in order to hold the town; but they left before the king came. At least a thousand barrels of wine and much in the way of other goods was found there. The town is larger than Lincoln. The next day the king continued his march, and lodged at an abbey, his army encamped in the villages around. Every day the men of arms spread out for twelve to fifteen miles, robbing and destroying, and they burnt a number of places. On the Monday and Tuesday, the king was on the move again, and lodged in villages. At midday on Wednesday he came up to the town of Caen, hearing that many men at arms were in the town. The king arrayed his battalions, and sent detachments to reconnoitre the town. They reported that there was a fine strong castle, garrisoned by the bishop of Bayeux, knights and men at arms. On this side of the river is the town, very large and fine, and at one end is a very noble abbey where William the Conqueror lies. It is walled round, with battlemented towers, and the defences are large and strong. There was no-one in the abbey. At the other end of the town is another noble abbey, for women. And there was no-one in either of the abbeys, nor in the town on this side of the river, except in the castle. All the townspeople had withdrawn into the part of the town beyond the river, where the constable of France was, and the chamberlain, de Tancarville, (who is a very great lord) and a number of people, perhaps five or six hundred, as well as the common townspeople. The common soldiers from our army, without leave or array, attacked the bridge, which had been well strengthened with a stockade and barriers, and they had a hard time of it; and the French defended the said bridge strongly, and offered a strong resistance before the bridge was taken. Then the said constable and chamberlain were taken, and up to a hundred knights, and 120 or 140 squires; and knights, squires and other townsmen were killed in great numbers in the streets, houses and gardens. It was impossible to know how many were men of substance because they were stripped and no-one could recognise them. None of our gentlemen were killed, except for one squire who was wounded and died two days later. And wine, food and other goods and chattels in great quantities were found in the town, which is larger than any in England except for London. And when the king left La Hogue, about two hundred ships stayed behind, which went to Roche Masse; and the sailors went ashore and burnt the countryside for five or six miles inland, taking goods back to their ships. Then they went to Cherbourg, where there is a fine town, a strong castle and a beautiful abbey; and they burnt the town and abbey. And they burnt everything along the sea coast from Roche Masse to Ouistreham on the Caen estuary, a distance of 120 miles. They burnt sixty-one warships with castles fore and aft, twenty-three fishing boats, and many other smaller vessels of 21 or 30 tons. The Thursday after the king arrived at Caen, the citizens of Bayeux asked the king if they could surrender themselves and their town to him and do homage; but he would not receive them for certain reasons until he was able to protect them from harm.

## b. Bartholomew Burghersh to John Stratford, archbishop of Canterbury, 29 July. (French)

Right reverend father in God and my most honoured lord, because I know that you would be very eager to have news of my lord the king and his exploits since he came to Normandy, I am writing to inform you that from the hour when he began his raid, he left La Hogue, where he landed, and went straight to Caen by way of the larger towns, Valognes, Carentan, St Lô and many others. But no-one of any great rank dared to await him, either in the towns, castles or countryside; they all fled, until the king came to Caen. At Caen there were the constable of France, the count d'Eu, the chamberlain, de Tancarville, and many knights, men at arms and common people from town and countryside, who had arrayed themselves in order to defend that town against the king and his whole army. But when the king arrived with his host and appeared before the town, the enemy withdrew beyond a bridge in the middle of the town and made a stand there. And when we came as close to the town as we could, the archers went straight to the bridge and attacked it with volleys of arrows. In the meanwhile some men at arms came up with them and attacked them fiercely; so that for fear of losses among our men, (because it was thought that there were no men at arms there but only the archers of the marshal, my lord Warwick) the king ordered them to retreat. And when my lord Warwick came to the bridge, he found them fighting hand to hand at the barriers, and they fought so well and nobly that they captured them to the last man, so that with our Lord's help our men won the bridge and thus entered the town and defeated the enemy. The constable of France surrendered to Sir Thomas Holland, with many knights and squires who were with him; and the chamberlain, de Tancarville, was captured by one of the prince's own knights, so he is the prince's prisoner. And between 120 and 140 noble and valiant knights were killed and captured, of whom about a hundred are still alive; and five thousand squires, citizens and commons were taken or killed. So far, our affairs have gone as well as possible, praised be the Lord! And the king stayed two or three days to provision his host from the town, which was full of supplies, and intends to march directly against his adversary, to bring matters to whatever end God may have decreed. Our ships came up to the end of the estuary leading to Caen, and have burnt or destroyed about a hundred vessels along the coast, as well as doing much damage in the country by burning and other means. That is all the news I have at the moment, my lord. May the Holy Spirit keep you in honourable estate, in good health and long life. Written at Caen, 29 July.

My lord the king has decided that all prisoners taken shall be sent to England, and shall not be released against ransoms or otherwise, until he has made more progress with his campaign.

## vi. Richard Wynkeley, 2 September. (Latin)

We must bless the God of heaven and confess his merits to all men living, for He has shown His mercy to us. For, after the battle at Caen, in which many were killed and the town taken and stripped to the bare walls, Bayeux freely surrendered, lest it should suffer the same fate. Our lord the king marched on Rouen; two cardinals came to him, and tried to open peace negotiations at Lisieux. They were received in courteous enough fashion, out of reverence for the Apostolic See and Holy Church; they were told that our lord the king, always anxious for peace, would seek it by all reasonable ways and means of which he knew, and he had offered many suggestions because of his desire for peace, even though it was much to the prejudice of his cause; he was now ready to treat for peace, if a reasonable offer was forthcoming. The said cardinals, after they had spoken to the king's adversary, came back later; and they offered the duchy of Aquitaine, as it had been held by his father, and held out hopes of a good marriage alliance if a peace could be arranged. But this was not acceptable, and the cardinals did not find the king's adversary in a mood to negotiate; so, despairing of success, they simply withdrew. The king, however, continued his march, taking all the great towns along his route; no-one resisted, and all the inhabitants fled. Thus God set such fear in them that it seemed that they lost heart. So a very few soldiers were able to take castles and fortresses, even though very strong, by a light attack. His adversary gathered a great army at Rouen, and even though it was very numerous, broke down the bridges across the Seine. He followed the king on the other side of the Seine, matching each day's march, and breaking down or strengthening all the bridges lest we should cross. Even though the whole countryside was laid waste for twenty miles around, and to within a mile of where he was, he neither wished nor dared to cross the Seine to defend his people and kingdom. And so our lord the king came to Poissy, where he found the bridge broken. And his adversary did not rest beyond Paris, but ordered 1000 horse and 2000 foot with mangonels to guard the said bridge and prevent its repair. He had all the bridges round Paris, by which we might have crossed, broken. When three or four beams had been put across the broken bridge, some archers crossed, though only few in number. They killed an estimated thousand men or thereabouts of the enemy, and put the rest to flight. When the bridge was repaired, the king marched into Picardy, and his adversary followed on his flank. Because the bridges were broken, our lord the king was unable to find a way across except in the tidal reach between Crotoy and Abbeville; here the whole army crossed unharmed at a place which none of the local people knew to be a safe ford except for six or ten people at a time. Our men crossed almost everywhere, as if it were a safe ford, much to the amazement of those who knew the place. And the king's adversary sent about 1000 horse and 5000 or more foot to guard the crossing and to resist the king; but the earl of Northampton and Sir Reginald Cobham with a hundred armed men and some archers, went in front of the main army and drove them off by force, killing that day two thousand or more; the rest fled to Abbeville, where the king's adversary and his army were. From there, our lord the king went towards Crécy, where his adversary came up with him in the fields; the latter had a very large army with him, estimated at 12,000 knights and 60,000 others under arms. The adversary himself, intending to attack the king personally, stationed himself in the front line; and he was opposed by the prince, who was in our front line. After a fierce and prolonged conflict, the adversary was twice driven off, and a third time, having gathered his men, the fighting was fiercely renewed. But, by the grace of God, two kings were killed in the battle: the king of Bohemia (for certain) and the king of Majorca (according to common report). Two archbishops were also killed, the archbishop of Sens and another whose name is unknown. In addition, the duke of Lorraine, the counts of Alençon, Blois, Flanders, Aumale, Beaumont (that is, John of Hainault) and Harcourt with his two sons, and six German counts were killed, besides numerous other barons and knights, whose names are not yet known; but according to the French prisoners, the flower of the whole knighthood of France has been killed. The king of France, so it is said, was wounded in the face by an arrow, and only just escaped. His standard bearer was killed in his sight, and his standard was torn to shreds. And, praise be Him who saves those who trust in Him, apart from two knights and a squire, the whole army is intact and unharmed; no nobles were killed, but only a few Welsh, not at the time, but later, because they exposed themselves foolishly to danger. Farewell in the name of Our Lord Jesus Christ and give thanks to God, Who had delivered our lord the king and his army from great danger. Written between Boulogne and Wissant, 2 September.

## vii. Edward III to Sir Thomas Lucy, 3 September. (French)

Edward by the grace of God king of England and France and Lord of Ireland to his dear and loyal knight Thomas Lucy, greeting. Because we know that you would be glad to have news of us, we are writing to say that we arrived at La Hogue near Barfleur on the twelfth of July last with all our men safe and sound, praise be to God; and we remained there to disembark our men and horses, and to provision the troops, until the following Tuesday, on which day we moved towards Valognes and took the castle and town. Then, continuing on our march, we had the bridge over the river Douve repaired which the enemy had broken down; and we crossed it and took the castle and town of Carentan. From there we went straight to St Lô and found the bridge at Pont-Hébert near this town destroyed in order to hinder our progress. We had it rebuilt at once; the next day we took the town, and made our way directly to Caen, without a single day's rest between our departure from La Hogue and our arrival there. As soon as we had encamped at Caen our men began to attack the town, which was very strong and filled with men at arms, about 1600 in all, as well as 30,000 armed common people who defended it and fought well and boldly, so that the struggle was very fierce and prolonged. But, praise be to God, the town was at last taken by force, without losing any of our men; and among the prisoners were the count of Eu, constable of France, and the chamberlain, Tancarville, (who had been proclaimed marshal of France that day), and about 140 other bannerets and knights, as well as many squires and rich citizens; and many noble knights and gentlemen were killed, and a great number of common people. Our fleet, which remained with us, burnt and destroyed the whole sea-coast from Harfleur up to the dyke at Colleville near Caen; and they burnt the town of Cherbourg and the ships in the harbour. In all over a hundred great ships and other enemy vessels have been burnt by us and our people. And then we rested for four days at Caen to provision and rest our army; and from there, because we had been assured that our enemy had come to Rouen, we made our way straight to him. As soon as he knew this, he broke the bridge at Rouen so that we could not cross, and at the same time we met two cardinals at the city of Lisieux. They made us stay there under pretext of negotiating a treaty but really in order to delay our march. However, we answered them briefly, saying that we would not lose a day for such reasons, though whenever justice was offered us we would be ready to make a proper answer. When we learnt that the bridge at Rouen was broken, we encamped on the river Seine, very close to Paris, and then continued our march along the said river. We found all the bridges broken or strengthened and defended, so that we were in no way able to cross to our enemy; nor did he wish to approach us, although he followed us each day along the other bank, and this greatly annoyed us. When we came to Poissy near Paris we found the bridge broken, and our adversary had established himself in Paris with all his men, and had demolished the bridge at St Cloud so that we could not cross to Paris from where we were.

So we stayed for three days at Poissy, as much to await the enemy in case he wished to give battle, as to engage in repairing the bridge. While the bridge was being repaired, a large enemy force appeared on the other bank to disturb the work, but before the bridge was rebuilt some of our men crossed on a beam and defeated them, killing many of them. And when we saw that our enemy did not want to come and give battle, we laid waste the countryside, skirmishing with the enemy each day. And we crossed the bridge with our army, and headed for Picardy, the better to draw our enemy into battle. When we came to the river Somme, we found the bridges broken, so we went towards St Valery to cross at a ford where the sea ebbs and flows. When we arrived a large number of men at arms and common people came to defend the crossing against us, but we crossed in spite of them by force of arms. By God's grace a thousand men crossed abreast where before this barely three or four used to cross, and so we and all our army crossed safely in an hour and a half. The enemy were defeated, and many were captured; a great many were killed without loss on our side. That same day, soon after we had crossed the river, our adversary appeared on the other bank with a very large force. He arrived so suddenly that we were not in the least ready; so we waited there and took up battle positions, and stayed like this the whole day and the next day, until the afternoon. Finally, when we saw that he did not want to cross but turned back to Abbeville, we marched towards Crécy to meet him on the other side of the forest. On Saturday 26 August when we arrived at Crécy our enemy appeared near us in the morning with a great number of men, for he had more than 12,000 men at arms, of whom eight thousand were gentlemen, knights and squires. So we drew up in battle array and waited on foot until mid-afternoon, when the two armies came together in the open field. The battle was very fierce and long drawn out, lasting from mid-afternoon until the evening. The enemy bore themselves nobly, and often rallied, but in the end, praise be to God, they were defeated and our adversary fled. There were killed the kings of Bohemia and Majorca (and other nobles) and many other counts and barons and other great lords, whose names are not yet known. In a small area where the first onslaught occurred more than 1500 knights and squires died, quite apart from many others who died later elsewhere on the field. After the victory we stayed there all night, fasting and without eating or drinking. The next morning we went in pursuit of the enemy, and killed more than 4000, men at arms, Genoese and other armed men. And our adversary, after his defeat, went to Amiens, where he had many of the Genoese killed, claiming that they had betrayed him. And it is reported that he is gathering a new army to attack us again, but we trust in God, and pray that He will continue his grace to us as He has done so far. And we have now moved towards the sea to get reinforcements and supplies from England, both of men at arms and equipment and other necessaries, because our marches have been long and continuous. But we do not expect to leave the kingdom of France until we have made an end of our war, with God's help. Given under our privy seal at Calais, 3 September 1346.

## viii. Michael Northburgh, 4 September. (French)

Greetings. This is to tell you that our lord the king came to Poissy on the eve of the Assumption of Our Lady (14 August), where there was a bridge across the river Seine, which was broken. But the king waited there until the bridge was rebuilt. While the bridge was being repaired, a large number of common people from the country-side around and from Amiens, all well armed, arrived. The earl of Northampton and his men attacked them, and more than 500 of our enemy were killed, thanks be to God; and the others fled on horse-back. On another occasion, our men crossed the river and killed many of the common people of France and of the town of Paris and elsewhere, well armed and from the French king's army; so that our men have made new, good bridges against our enemy, thanks be to God, without loss or great damage to them. And on the day after the Assumption our lord the king crossed the river Seine and went to Poix, a strong walled town, with a very strong castle inside; and it was held by the enemy. When the vanguard and centre had passed the town, the rearguard attacked the town and took it; and more than 300 enemy men at arms were killed. The next day the earl of Suffolk and Sir Hugh Despenser attacked the common people of the country, who had gathered and were well armed; and they defeated them and killed 200 or more; and they took more than sixty gentle-men prisoner. And then the king marched to Grandvilliers; and just as they had taken up quarters there, the vanguard was challenged by men at arms from the king of Bohemia's household. And our men rushed out and fought them, but were beaten to the ground; but, thanks be to God, Lord Northampton went out and rescued the knights and other men, so that no-one was killed or captured, except Thomas Talbot. He pursued the enemy to within two miles of Amiens and took eight men at arms, killing twelve. The rest were well mounted and fled to Amiens. And then the king of England, who God preserve, marched towards Ponthieu on St Bartholomew's day (24 August) and came to the river Somme, which flows into the sea from Abbeville in Ponthieu. The king of France had posted 500 men at arms and 3000 armed common people to guard the crossing; and thanks be to God, the king of England and his army forded the river Somme where no-one had crossed it before, without losing any men. They engaged the enemy and killed more than 2000 armed men; and the remainder were pursued right up to the gates of Abbeville, and a large number of knights and squires taken. That same day Sir Hugh Despenser took Crotoy and he and his men killed four hundred men at arms and held the town, which they found full of provisions. That night the king of England encamped in the forest of Crécy, on the river bank, because the king of France appeared on the other side after we had crossed; but he did not wish to cross over to us, and returned towards Abbeville. The following Friday the king of England encamped once again in the forest of Crécy. On the Saturday morning, he set out towards Crécy, and there the scouts of our lord the king found the king of France approaching us with four large battalions, and surveyed the enemy strength. As God so willed it, his army met ours in the open field a little before vespers, and the battle was very fierce and long drawn out, because the enemy bore themselves nobly. (A list of the dead follows.) And Philip of Valois and the marquis called the Emperor-elect scarcely escaped, so men said. The total of good men at arms killed on the field that day, apart from commoners and footsoldiers, was reckoned at 1542. That night the king of England and his whole army remained on the battlefield in arms. The next morning, before sunrise, another battalion, large and strong, came up to us. The earl of Northampton and the earls of Norfolk and Warwick went out and defeated them, and took a large number of knights and squires, killing more than 2000 and pursuing them for some miles. That night the king encamped at Crécy, and the next morning marched to Boulogne, taking Étaples on his march. From there he marched to Calais. From what I have heard, he intends to besiege Calais. For this reason the king has sent to you for supplies, to be sent as quickly as possible; because since we left Caen we have lived off the countryside with great difficulty and much harm to our men, but, thanks be to God, without losses. But we are now in such a plight that part of our needs must be met by supplies. Written before Calais, 4 September.

# 2. The acts of war of Edward III (1346)

This day-to-day diary of the Crécy campaign survives in only one manuscript (Corpus Christi College, Cambridge MS 170), which is a late-fourteenth-century copy. Four leaves are missing in the centre of the quire, and at the end the copyist has repeated an entire page. (It is possible that multiple copies were being made, and the copyist broke off when he found that he had mistakenly entered his second copy in the wrong quire.) The result is a tantalising fragment: had the manuscript been complete, it might well have given us a vivid and first-hand account of the battle itself, as the standard of writing is generally of a high order. Copies of the full manuscript seem to have been used by two other chroniclers, at the abbeys of Malmesbury in Wiltshire and Meaux in Yorkshire, and some of the missing material can be retrieved from their summaries, though they both pass over the battle very briefly.

The accuracy of the diary can be checked against the so-called Kitchen Journal, the accounts of the king's kitchen entered in the royal household accounts, where each halt of the royal household is noted. There is almost complete agreement between the two sources, particularly when the division of the army into three battalions, marching up to ten miles apart, is taken into account. There are indications in the text that the writer of the diary was with the prince's division, whose actions are always given prominence, but we have no clue as to his identity. The diary was probably written up from rough notes, as the style is reasonably polished, if sometimes idiosyncratic. The inclusion of the texts of two letters between Edward III and Philip of Valois would point to someone attached to the prince's council, with access to such documents; it seems unlikely that the writer was on the king's council, as he has nothing to say about the tactical discussions such as the change of direction at the very beginning of the expedition, which we learn from elsewhere.

# The acts of war of Edward III (1346)

*These are the acts of war of the most illustrious prince lord Edward, by grace of God king of England and France and of Edward the eldest son of that king, prince of Wales, duke of Cornwall and earl of Chester, which they did at sea and in the kingdom of France, from the last day of June 1346 onwards.*

King Edward's journey to the English coast was without mishap. Here he gathered a famous and unconquered army of nobles, knights and commons and a fleet of ships terrible to both the eye and the mind of the enemy, in order to enforce his hereditary rights in the kingdom of France, which was his by right of his mother. And when they had assembled from all parts of England at Portsmouth and in the places nearby, men, horses and all the necessary victuals for them were got ready to go on board ship. When the necessary victuals had been taken on board, and when a fair-sized company of ships had gathered, the king anchored off the Isle of Wight, opposite the town of Yarmouth, and waited for three days for the rest of the fleet.

The nobles of the army, who had been left behind, knowing that the king was at Yarmouth, set out in one squadron on 5 July. More ships gathered daily, until they stretched as far as the mouth of the haven of the island, called the Needles; and they were about to set out, when the wind suddenly changed to the opposite quarter. So the king recalled them altogether because of this, and they quickly broke off their journey and returned to Portsmouth where they tried each day to reach the open sea.

The sailors weighed anchor on the eleventh of July, and the ships gathered at sea as the king ordered. None of them knew in which part of the world they would slacken the ropes, but our Lord helped the king of England, and the winds and tides were favourable. They landed safely on the island of St Marcouf, in the port of La Hogue.

At dawn on the 12th, the inhabitants of the island woke to bitter and disturbing news. When they saw the terrible sight of the ships, as I afterwards learnt, they fled from the enemy king as quickly as they could to caves and woods, leaving all their possessions. At noon, the king and his army landed on the shore, and in a group made their way to a high hill near the shore, where Edward prince of Wales, William Montagu, Roger Mortimer, William le Ros, Roger de la Warre and Richard de la Vere and various others of their

27

company were knighted by the king. Then the soldiers dispersed in all directions, slaying enemy footsoldiers and burning excellent towns and manor-houses. At the same time fourteen ships, well fitted out for an attack on England by the enemy, which were found lying on the shore, were burnt with all their gear. The king and his company climbed a higher hill, for strategic reasons, from which he could weigh up the appearance of the whole countryside. Then they went down to look for suitable lodgings, and settled on a little village two miles from the port. But as the earl of Warwick was going to the lodgings with one of his squires, some of the enemy, hiding in a certain wood, rushed on him unawares and very violently, so that he thought that he would certainly be captured. But before the enemy could rejoice in their first victory over the English, he recovered his spirits, and, though mounted on a poor horse, he and his squire fought back boldly and he killed some of the attackers. The rest, fearing that they too would be killed, and thinking that there was not one Englishman but a thousand, took to their heels with all speed. And who could deny that the Almighty went before the English king and his army on their march, and made things easy for them, when five hundred Genoese, sent by the king's adversary to protect that port, had spent ten weeks continuously on the coast, and had only left three days before he landed, because the enemy were short of money, and went elsewhere. In the meanwhile, Robert Bertram, constable of France, summoned the nobles and great men of the peninsula, and all those below a certain age, to arm themselves on behalf of the king's adversary and resist the attack on their country, naming the twelfth as the day of assembly. But seeing the English fleet, a guest they did not want to greet, they fled in haste, leaving the way into Normandy clear for the king and the English army.

On the 13th, a mass of supplies for both men and horses were unloaded from the ships, and the enemy did not offer any hindrance. Those who stayed on board that day and night felt that they were obedient and unlucky, because the rest cheerfully and boldly set fire to the countryside around, until the sky itself glowed with a fiery colour. However, the English king, feeling for the sufferings of the poor people of the country, issued an edict throughout the army, that no house or manor was to be burnt, no church or holy place sacked, and no old people, children or women in his kingdom of

France were to be harmed or molested; nor were they to threaten any other people except men who resisted them, or do any kind of wrong, on pain of life or limb. He also ordered that if anyone caught someone in the act of doing these or other criminal acts and brought him to the king, he should have a reward of forty shillings.

The English, eager to make war on the enemy, ranged across various parts of the country on the 14th, and several reached the town of Barfleur, where they found an abundance of hidden riches and returned unharmed with a number of prisoners, both citizens and peasants. But they first burnt the town, and seven curiously fitted-out warships as well, which they found in the port. The army ravaged in a similar fashion on the 15th, 16th and 17th; the English king appointed the earl of Northampton constable, and the earl of Warwick marshal of the army, to check the rashness of the troops. Then they divided the army into three divisions: the vanguard under the prince of Wales, the centre under the king, and the rearguard under the bishop of Durham. In the vanguard, the following raised their banners: the earls of Northampton and of Warwick, Bartholomew de Burghersh the elder, John Verdoun, John Mohoun, Thomas Oughtred, John Fitzwalter, William Kerdeston, Reginald Say, Robert Bourchier, William de St Amand and others. In the centre, the earl of Oxford, Edward Montagu, Richard Talbot, Reginald Cobham, Robert Ferrers, John Darcy the younger, Thomas Bradeston, John Darcy the elder, John Gray, Eble Straunge, Michael Poynings, Maurice Berkeley, John Stirling, Peter Breauce, John Chevereston, Butler of Wemme, Godfrey d' Harcourt, who did homage for his lands and possessions in the duchy of Normandy to the English king at La Hogue, William Wildesby, Walter Wetewang, John Thoresby, Philip Weston. In the rearguard, the earls of Arundel, Suffolk, and Huntingdon, Hugh Despenser, Robert Morley, James Audley, John Grey, Thomas Astley, Robert Colville, John Sutton, William Cantilupe, Gerard Delisle, John Straunge, John Bolord. With the army divided in this way by the king's counsel, and with everything prepared in the correct fashion, the king began his journey into Normandy on the eighteenth of July, very eager to encounter the enemy. By thickly wooded and very narrow roads, the army reached the town of Valognes, a rich and worthy place, without harm or mishap. The inhabitants of the town came out and threw themselves at the king's feet, asking him only to spare their lives; the king most mercifully admitted them to his peace, and ordered his earlier edict to be repeated, with the same penalties and rewards. The king lodged in the house of the dukes of Normandy, while the prince stayed in the house of the bishop of Coutances.

On the 19th, some evildoers left the army who were not afraid of breaking the king's edict, and set fire to everything near the road. The English army left the fine town of Montebourg to one side, and unharnessed at Saint Côme du Mont. Here they heard rumours that (the bridge nearby) had been broken down by the retreating enemy, hoping to hinder the king's progress. The causeway was narrow and the water very deep, too deep to ford. Nor could the king find any other place for his army to cross: so he put Reginald Cobham, John Stirling, Roger Mortimer, Hugh Despenser and Bartholomew de Burghersh the younger in charge of the bridge and causeway, so that both could be repaired and strengthened as necessary by the carpenters.

On the 20th, the king and his army crossed the bridge and causeway safely, and came to the town of Carentan, surrounded by running water and marshes, and embellished by a fairly strong castle, but the footsoldiers who had gone on ahead, devoured a large amount of food, regardless of danger and ignoring the harm it might do to the army. It was very strictly ordered in the king's name that no-one should waste more food than he needed, the penalties and rewards to be as in the previous edict. The king stayed the night here, and the prince passed the night in the aforesaid castle. After they had crossed the bridge, leaving the island of St Marcouf behind, they now reached the borders of Normandy. The king and his army crossed four bridges in the marsh already mentioned, and followed a narrow causeway. They pitched their tents at Pont-Hebert, after a longer day's journey than usual. The bridge into Normandy, broken down by the retreating enemy, was repaired by the prince of Wales that day, but no-one was able to cross it until the morning, when all the vanguard was to go over: for the king had heard that Robert Bertram and others of the enemy were not far from his army, and did not want to lose any of his men while they could be defended. The vanguard crossed on the twenty-second and climbed to the top of a nearby hill, and drew themselves up in battle array against a possible

enemy attack, which, they hoped, was imminent. Here Henry de
Burghersh was knighted by the prince of Wales. These lords entered
St Lô, a walled town with a castle, together that night, where there
was plenty of food of all kinds. The Constable and Marshal of France
and others of the enemy had sheltered here the previous night. At
the dawn trumpet-call on the 23rd, the king ordered the army to
gather at Torigny, but new information reached him, and he suddenly changed his plans and set out in a different direction to
Cormolain. The enemy had also been here the previous night. Those
who were responsible for quartering the English army at Torigny,
reserving houses for the nobles, learnt of the army's retreat and,
setting fire to town and countryside, hastened to the king, coming
to him in small groups from all over the countryside.

As they left Cormolain on the 24th, they burnt the town and
surrounding country so that the enemy should know of their coming.
But some of the archers, trusting in their own strength and despite
the king's edict, were suffocated when the building which they were
sacking was set on fire by enemies lying in wait. The army encamped
at St Germain d'Ectot that night. On the 25th the king came to
Fontenay-le-Pesnel, the prince going towards Cheux. For the king
heard that his way was blocked, and he could only continue by
giving battle. All the men who had fled from him in Normandy had
assembled in the splendid town of Caen, in order to block the way
of the king and his army. The king, bearing in mind the Saviour's
sacrifice, sent brother Geoffrey of Maldon, of the order of St
Augustine and professor of theology, with letters to the enemy
urging the town and castle of Caen to surrender. If they did so,
they could keep all their goods and the town would be unharmed.
But they refused to allow him to return to the king, and put him in
chains in the castle of Caen. This wicked action of the French in not
sending back the messenger, meant that their own punishment was
all the more severe. For on the 26th, when the messenger had not
returned, the prince and his troops, awoken by trumpets at dawn,
set fire to their lodgings, torchbearers ran everywhere, doing their
duty, until wherever one looked, you could see bright fire. The
prince commanded his own lords; they all approached Caen at the
same time, with the keepers of the wagons and carts following the
vanguard, so that as they crossed the fields, the number of men in

the army should seem to be greater. The king's troops approached the town: the helmets of the lords, their banners and well-armed horses made a fine show. He who did the best deeds of arms on the way would certainly be least blamed or slandered. The rearguard followed, and took up position on hills on the four sides of the town, their lances raised and banners boldly displayed, hoping to find a good place for an attack. The town had a very well fortified castle, fine churches and houses, newly strengthened on one side by a moat and foursquare wooden walls, on the other defended by marshes, a stone wall and the sea, an arm of which divided the town, with a strong bridge over it. It seemed impossible to take to ordinary eyes. But the king was strengthened by the justice of his cause, and the prince, showing his power in his father's least quarrel, attacked the town with his troops and found no resistance to his entrance.

The prince at once seized the abbey for himself and his following: here Matilda the good, once queen of England, is buried. The king occupied a suitable manor-house in the suburbs of the town, and the rearguard pitched their tents. The enemies of the English sent his men in safety to the town, as described below. The bishop of Bayeux who tore up the king's letters, as will appear below, and detained the messenger, guarded the castle with the help of four barons and two hundred men at arms and a hundred Genoese cross-bowmen. Men at arms and a number of Genoese were sent, in thirty boats kept ready in the harbour, to guard the tidal causeway against the English, while the rest of the knights promised to keep watch on the bridge already mentioned, which they strengthened with heavy barriers. The townsmen carried all their goods to that part of the town, thinking that they were well defended against the English; and almost half the town was deserted. At about eight o'clock, as already mentioned, the prince entered the town: after everyone had been allocated a lodging, and the army had been fed from the abundant stores of meat and drink, and everything had been made ready again, the earl of Warwick with a modest company of men at arms set out for the bridge in order to deal with the enemy archers and the other Norman soldiers there.

The earl of Northampton and Sir Richard Talbot followed him, but when they saw the enemy, they did not hold themselves back any longer, but rushed on the enemy and exerted themselves against them with loud cries. Troops laid in ambush joined in the battle; the earl soon found his match, and knights fought hand to hand around the supports of the bridge, dealing grievous blows. The commanders ran to and fro, organising the crossing of archers and Welshmen by the ford: the enemy men-at-arms and Genoese detailed to guard the ford resisted them, hurling spears and quarrels at them. The archers burnt two of the enemy boats in the harbour entrance. As the struggle went on for a long while at the bridge, and more and more English troops arrived, the French turned and fled to the houses and upper rooms. The earls and other leaders followed, slaying on all sides. The rest of the ships fled, and the English crossed the river in light boats, killing everyone they caught. Those who had taken refuge in the houses, seeing so many of their countrymen killed and death imminent, surrendered to their pursuers, but the footsoldiers of the English army killed nobles and lesser men alike, without allowing anyone to ransom themselves. However the English did return with a number of noble captives. And those who could carry away booty came back with a vast amount of treasure from the houses. The count of Eu, who promised either to hold the town against the king of England's enemies for forty days or to fight for the king in the field, was captured there by Sir Thomas Holland. The count of Tancarville was captured by Sir Thomas Daniel, one of the prince of Wales' retinue, and a number of other nobles likewise. There were 95 captives and over 2500 slain, apart from those killed in pursuit across the fields. Nor did anyone make a sortie out of the castle during the battle. The king made a proclamation throughout the army that no-one was to imprison women, children or clergy or to ransack churches or houses, on the same penalties as before. In the first English attack on the town, three or four of the higher houses near the bridge were set on fire, and burned brightly all night. The bishop remained ensconced in the castle on the 27th, but five servants came out at daybreak; they were ambushed by the English guarding that sector, who pursued them and killed three of them. Two were led to the king, who told him who was in the castle and about the seizure of Geoffrey of Maldon, the messenger mentioned earlier, how his letters were torn up and everything else about it, insisting that it was true that the bishop of Bayeux had torn up the letters, and had cruelly imprisoned the said Geoffrey. They also said that the garrison of the castle of Caen would surrender if it was not for the stubborn resistance of the said bishop. The English eagerly returned to the work of despoiling the town, only taking jewels, clothing or precious ornaments because of the abundance. The English sent their booty to their ships. The ships from La Hogue followed them along the shore, and had burnt towns, manors and more than a hundred ships gathered from different ports to help the enemies of the English. They were now only nine miles away at most and were preparing to inform the king of England of their own successes. They found such a mass of goods sent to them that they could not transport all the spoils from Caen and elsewhere. On the 28th, nothing more was done, except that the countryside was set on fire all round, so that at least the men were not idle for lack of work. An indescribable fear seized men throughout the countryside, and on the 29th, fifteen of the greatest citizens of Bayeux came to surrender that town to the king, travelling under a safe conduct.

*Four pages of the manuscript are missing here. Some of the details of what happened in the interval can be provided from the chronicle of the monastery of Malmesbury, probably based on a complete copy of the same text:*

The king retreated from Caen, leaving a few men in the district, and set out towards Normandy, laying waste as he went. He made a detour towards Troarn, where he found neither men nor women. But when he came to Lisieux, which his men took and sacked, he met two cardinals, sent by the pope, whom the Welsh troops robbed of twenty great horses. He remained there for a whole day, out of respect for the Lord's day and for the cardinals, listening to their sermons on peace and concord; they also offered him Gascony and Ponthieu to be held of the French king just as his father had held them, if he would make peace. The king thought that their mission was a waste of time, and, after restoring the horses stolen by the Welsh, sent them back with a safe conduct to the papal court. The bridges over the Seine, however, had been broken by the Normans; nonetheless, the Welsh swam across and killed many Normans, returning safely and bringing with them some little boats. In these some of the English men at arms crossed and killed at least 105

Normans, who had often exposed their backsides at the English.★

The king crossed the neck of a bend in the river Seine, taking his whole army across country where no-one had ever travelled before. The English army fiercely attacked a castle on the river; here Richard Talbot and Thomas Holland were wounded.

*The text of the Corpus manuscript now resumes:*

On the same day, Robert de Ferrers, taking his men with him, crossed the Seine secretly in a small boat and attacked the very strong castle at La Roche Guyon. The enemy resisted them, but they entered the outer bailey, and took the second by a violent assault. The garrison, terrified by the assaults, grew faint-hearted and surrendered the castle and themselves as prisoners at the mercy of the said Sir Robert. Sir Edward Attewoode was killed here. The castle was full of noble ladies, whom he released unharmed without shame or injury. Taking an oath that they would pay ransoms from the captured knights and squires, he sent them back unharmed to the castle, and returned to the English army to tell the king of this happy event. More than forty Normans were killed or captured that day. The prince spent the night at Mousseaux while the king was at Freneuse. The cardinals of Naples and Clermont came back on the subject of a peace treaty and mutual alliance with the English, but because the treaty was not to the liking of the English, they returned to the enemy that night, having got a light-hearted answer from the English. The countryside was burnt on all sides on the eleventh of the month.

The English army, leaving the town of Mantes (where the vanguard of the French army was encamped) to one side, seized Aubergenville in Ile-de-France (?). The earls of Northampton and Warwick with a moderate company of men at arms set out towards the fine town of Meulan, equipped, like Caen, with strong walls and a moat, to see if the English army could cross the Seine by the bridge of the said town. But they could not complete the task, because the bridge had in front of it a tower which was impossible to capture, filled with men at arms and crossbowmen to defend it. The safe position of the enemy as well as their scorn and insults

★ Probably a taunt alluding to the common French story of the period that the English had tails.

made the English furious, and they could not restrain themselves from attacking the tower. Some of the defenders were killed by the English arrows, and some of the leaders of the English army were wounded by quarrels. The English saw that the bridge was broken down nearer the town, and returned to the English king's army, the worse for their wounds. However, no English were killed in the battle. And although the enemy were opposite the English army, and could have chosen various places at which to cross the river, they never showed themselves nor offered battle.

At dawn on the 12th, the English armed themselves and raised fire-signals everywhere to encourage the enemy to attack and cross boldly at that point. From gleams of light and ashes they knew that the flower of the French army were on the opposite bank; but Philip, guessing that if the English crossed the river, they would make for Paris, feared the wrath of the townspeople. He knew that he probably could not defend the Pont-de-Poissy against the English, because the wall, although fairly strong, had not been reinforced. With tears in his eyes, he ordered his sister the prioress and nuns of the order of St Dominic (who served Christ in seclusion there), and every one else in the town to leave, and to break down the bridge as they left, as I learned afterwards. So in accordance with the orders of the so-called king, when they had broken down the bridge they all fled with his army to Paris. Fearing the arrival of the English, he arranged that if the English came, the walls and gates were to be ruined. The French also prepared various siege-machines in case the English arrived and started to besiege the town the next day. But the king made his way to Fresnes, and the prince to Bures, from which the English could see the city of Paris as well as most of the Ile-de-France. The king and the army took an easy journey on the 13th, towards Poissy, knowing that the bridge across the Seine there was broken. The king ordered his carpenters to repair it without delay. The king lodged in the newly built royal palace next to the very fine priory in the town; the prince stayed in the old palace of the king of France. The priory of the town was empty when the inhabitants were driven within its doors by fear at the arrival of the king and of the rest of the English. It had a very fine church, that seemed as if built in one day, ornamented with most splendid altars and images. Even the outbuildings were built of squared and planed

beams and quarried stones. Nowhere in the world would you find
a finer priory than this, and indeed I confess that the workmanship
of it was better than the palace in which the king stayed. In the
afternoon, when wood was found for the carpenters to repair the
bridge – and they had only put a beam across the broken part – a
squadron of the enemy were seen boldly approaching the bridge at
great speed. The English at once armed themselves to rush against
the enemy, but no-one crossed the bridge except by the beam in
question, which was sixty feet long and a foot wide and very difficult
to cross. But despite the danger, they met the enemy, for twenty-
five banners were raised and unfurled at the foot of the bridge. The
French came on in order, like a ravening wolf on the sheepfold.
They separated the English force for a time, but seeing that they
could not hold out against the English any longer, the French
turned and fled, followed by the English footsoldiers as far as they
could, who put to death anyone they captured. None of the English
army were killed in the skirmish. Some of them, to escape more
quickly from the English, took the horses from the carts used to bring
supplies to the garrison of the bridge and, two or three to a horse,
escaped from the English. But five hundred or more French lay dead
on the field. The English found twenty-one carts with stone shot and
quarrels as well as supplies (which they removed) and these they set
on fire. They returned to the main body of the army, bringing with
them weapons and various French standards. On the same day the
bridge was repaired, so that a horse and cart could safely cross it.
On the 14th, rumours ran through the army that the enemy were
lurking in the very strong city of Paris, and the king remained where
he was on that day and the next waiting for the appearance of the
enemy, which he heartily hoped to see. On the same day, the finest
places of the kingdom of France, that is, the castle of Montjoie and a
most excellent palace completed by Philip de Valois within the last
two years called Chastel le Roy, which he preferred to all others, as
well as the town of St Germain-en-Laye with another palace of the
French king and all the countryside around to within two miles of
Paris, were burnt almost at the same time. In the evening, the king
had it proclaimed throughout the army that no raiding or burning
was to be done the next day, because it was the Feast of the Assumption of the Blessed Virgin, on pain of the usual penalties; instead

everyone was to make their devotions to the Mother of God; nor did anything happen on that day which was worth recording. On the 16th the king and his army went safely across the bridge at Poissy, after setting fire to the French king's palace in which the prince of Wales had stayed. The priory and the other palace were put in the care of some of his ministers by the king. And then they left the bridge they had repaired in the broken state in which they found it. The countryside was burnt as far as Moleaux in Normandy, where the king stayed. The prince, however, stayed at Grisy-les Platres near the fine town of Pontoise. The king sent an answer to the letters of his enemy (which had been brought to him at Auteuil, and which he had not answered) by the archbishop of Besançon, in which he said: 'Philip of Valois, we have read your letters by which you tell us that you wish to fight us and all our forces, between St Germain-des-Pres and Valgiral-de-les-Paris or between Franconville and Pontoise on Thursday, Saturday, Sunday or Tuesday next, as long as we and our men do no damage, burning or robbery. On this we let it be known to you that with God's assurance and in the clear right which we have to the crown of France which you wrongfully hold, to our disinheritance against God and right, we have come without pride or presumption to our kingdom of France, making our way to you to put an end to the war. But although you could have a battle with us, you break down the bridges between you and us, so that we cannot come near you or cross the river Seine. When we came to Poissy and repaired the bridge there which you had broken, we stayed three days, waiting for you and the army which you have gathered. You could have come there from any direction, as you wished, and because we could not get you to give battle, we decided to continue further into our kingdom, to comfort our loyal friends and punish rebels, whom you wrongly claim as your subjects; and we wish to remain in our kingdom without leaving it to carry on the war to our advantage as best we can, to the damage of our adversaries. Therefore, if you wish (as your letters indicate) to do battle with us in order to spare those whom you call your subjects, let it now be known that at whatever hour you approach you will find us ready to meet you in the field, with God's help, which thing we most earnestly desire for the common good of Christendom, since you will not accept or offer any reasonable terms for peace. But we shall never be dictated to by you, nor will we accept a day and place for battle on the conditions which you have named. Auteuil, 17 August, 1346.'

The prince of Wales obtained the village of Vessencourt as a gift for himself and his men.

On the 18th of the month, the king and his army approached a city in Picardy, which they were to pass by. The prince and his squadron stayed too long in front of the city, and indeed he dearly wanted to obtain permission for his men to attack from his father the king. But he did not dare to carry it out, for the king told him that he was likely to meet the enemy shortly, and he did not want to lose any men in such an attack. The king moved towards Milly, and after he had passed in front of that town, reached Troissereux safely with his squadron. On the 19th, in the morning, as the army went through the middle of the town of Oudeuil, where there was a castle to the west of the town . . . where the lord of the castle with his wife and household had stayed the previous night. Nor did they leave when the army arrived, but submitted to the mercy of the English. While the town and surrounding countryside were burnt, the king and prince reached the abbey of Sommereux. On the 20th, the English crossed at Camps-en-Amienois. The king ended his day's journey there, but the prince stayed at Molliens-Vidame. However, the town of Poix, which was surrounded by a stone wall and had a very strong castle . . . was attacked by the vanguard of the English army. But the king's messengers arrived and told the men at arms attacking it not to make any further attacks. They retreated a little, and when the messengers had gone, returned to their work, attacking the town more fiercely than usual. In the meanwhile the messengers returned and found the English digging mines; but the English were afraid of breaking the king's command in the presence of the messengers, and stopped their attack. But when the messengers had gone away again, they launched a very fierce assault. The townsmen defended the town with bows and mangonels and stones thrown from the ramparts; on the other side, several of their missiles demolished walls and gates. In the end the English set up scaling ladders, and because the defenders had been wounded by English arrows, the English were able to capture the walls on all sides. And so the English got into the town; but any fleeing men of Picardy whom they caught, they put to death without ransom. They approached the castle of the town, and applied blazing torches to its gate; but as soon as the men of Picardy hiding in the castle were attacked, they yielded the castle and its contents to the English. The English entered and took a number of prisoners, including some women and children, and found a quantity of goods, both from the town and the surrounding countryside, including horses and fine jewellery. For whoever wanted spoils could find them there to take. And the prince of Wales gave the men at arms and archers and servants of his household . . . (*Here the manuscript breaks off*)

# 3. Geoffrey le Baker: Chronicle

Geoffrey le Baker came from Swinbrook in Oxfordshire, and wrote his chronicle about 1357–60. We know very little about him, except that he may have been an acquaintance of Adam Murimuth, whose chronicle is a very valuable source for the early years of Edward III's reign, and that he probably wrote his own chronicles for Sir Thomas de la More, a local landowner and MP, who had played a minor part in securing Edward II's abdication. Like Murimuth, who was attached to the royal household, Baker seems to have had good contacts in high places, but he does not quote original documents in the same way as Murimuth and Robert Avesbury, who continued Murimuth's chronicle. Instead, he prefers to rewrite them, though as far as we can tell, he is respectful towards his sources, and his alterations consist largely of questions of style: he writes a Latin, which, if not strictly classical in its constructions, contains relatively few non-classical words. He also has a fondness for rhetoric at moments of high drama: compare the dry, terse narrative of the day's marches of the 1355 expedition, where he is clearly using a campaign diary, to the rhodomontades and technicolor details of the battle of Poitiers. Yet his actual account of the battle of Poitiers is the best single account we have.

His account of Crécy, written at a longer interval of time, is less satisfactory, but it preserves a number of details not found elsewhere, which are plainly authentic. It also gives, in more prosaic and realistic form, some of the episodes embroidered by Froissart, such as the king's meagre response to the request for aid from the prince's companions at the height of the battle. He does not mention the flock of crows and the thunderstorm which is supposed to have spoiled the crossbowmen's bowstrings, probably because they were exaggerated accounts of minor incidents. Another early writer, Giovanni Villani, says that two crows flew over the battlefield, and there was a light shower of rain. Villani's information came from the crossbowmen themselves; someone on the English side might well have failed to notice either event.

The account of the successful defence of Calais which follows is interesting as an example of a chivalrous exploit described by a writer who has no particular interest in the chivalrous implications of the affair. We see in Baker's account how Edward III's genius for good tactical planning was almost ruined by his foolhardy pursuit of the enemy, and how he saved the day by a return to skilled and prudent generalship.

# i. The battle of Crécy

On the evening of the following Friday, as the king was encamped on the bank of the Somme, Philip of Valois, the French usurper, came up on the other bank, where the English had crossed earlier; with him were the kings of Bohemia and Majorca, and an innumerable army, divided into eight great battalions. The French called out insolent challenges to the king and the English, and knights jousted in warlike fashion in the ford and on the banks. The king sent a message to the usurper, offering a peaceful and unharmed crossing of the ford if he wished to come and choose a place for a battle; but this timid Philip, who had earlier threatened to pursue the king, now refused battle, but turned away as if to cross the river elsewhere; and the king awaited him all night. The next day, Saturday, the king moved his army to the field of Crécy, where the usurper's army met him. So the king, always ready for battle, put the prince of Wales in charge of his first battalion, appointed commanders for the second, and kept the third under his own command; and he commended all things to God and the Blessed Virgin, having ensured that all his men awaited the enemy attack on foot, and having kept back the warhorses with his supply train for use in pursuit of the retreating enemy.

The French army was divided into nine battalions. The first was commanded by the king of Bohemia, a man of great wisdom and experience of warfare, who to preserve his reputation had asked the usurper for the command of the front line, and prophesied that he would die fighting against the most noble soldier in the world; for he was reproached for being foolish when he said that the king of England would not flee, and so begged insistently for command of the front line. The heroes on the French side were so confident in the numbers of their army that individuals asked for specific men on the English side as their prisoners. The king of Majorca asked for the English king to be given to him, while others asked for the prince or the earl of Northampton or others among those who seemed most noble: but the cunning usurper, fearing that his men would spend their whole time trying to capture nobles for ransom, and would only fight half-heartedly for a general victory, ordered the standard called the Oriflamme★; when this was raised, no-one was to take prisoners on pain of death. It was called the Oriflamme to imply that the mercy of the French was entirely consumed, and no-one's life could be spared, just as flaming oil destroys everything that can be burnt.

The standard to the right of the French king's position had on it broad gold fleurs-de-lis woven in gold thread at each side of the standard of the kings of France, which hung as if in an empty space. On the other side the English king ordered his standard to be unfurled, on which a dragon was depicted clothed in his arms; hence it was called the dragon standard, implying that the wildness of the leopard and the gentleness of the lilies would be turned into the dragon's cruelty.

So the troops stood drawn up in the field from mid-morning until mid-afternoon, while the threatening size of the French army was continually increased by new reinforcements. However, as the sun began to set, the first line of battle of the army advanced, trumpets and cornets sounding, drums and kettledrums rolling; and the noise of the French troops seemed like thunder to the English. The French crossbowmen began the attack; their crossbow bolts did not reach the English, however, but fell a long way off. Much to the terror of the crossbowmen, the English archers began to pick off their closely-packed enemies with arrows, and they ended the hail of crossbow bolts with a rain of arrows. Realising that the crossbow-men were not harming the English, the French men at arms, mounted on young warhorses and agile chargers, rode down seven thousand of the crossbowmen who were between them and the English, charging headlong into the English ranks in order to display their prowess. So a great cry went up from the victims trampled by the French cavalry, which those in the rear of the French army took to

★ Baker calls it the 'Oliflamme'.

43

be dying English troops. Every Frenchman strove to follow those who had already charged; foremost in such rashness and boldness were newly made knights, of whom there were a good number in the army, all eager to gain the glory which they thought they would earn by fighting the English king.

The English, on the other hand, calling on Christ's mother, made that Saturday holy with fasts. They quickly dug a large number of pits in the ground near their front line, each a foot deep and a foot wide, so that if the French cavalry approached, their horses would stumble in the pits. The archers were also assigned a place apart from the men at arms, so that they were positioned at the sides of the army almost like wings; in this way they did not hinder the men at arms, nor did they meet the enemy head on, but could catch them in their cross-fire.

Thus a great cry went up, as has been said, from the crossbow-men trampled by the cavalry and from the horses wounded by arrows, while the French line of battle was badly disordered by stumbling horses. When they attacked the well armed English, they were cut down with swords and spears, and many were crushed to death, without a mark on them, in the middle of the French army, because the press was so great. In this desperate battle, Edward of Woodstock, the king's eldest son, aged sixteen, displayed marvellous courage against the French in the front line, running through horses, felling knights, crushing helmets, cutting lances apart, avoiding the enemy's missiles; as he did so, he encouraged his men, defended himself, helped fallen friends to their feet, and set everyone an example; nor did he rest from his labours until the enemy retreated leaving behind a heap of dead bodies. There he learnt that knightly skill which he later put to excellent use at the battle of Poitiers, where he captured the French king. In this battle a handful of men in the front line held their ground together with the prince, whom the French repeatedly attacked, fresh troops coming up to replace the dead, weary, and wounded; so the prince and his companions were kept continually at work by these new attacks, and were forced to their knees by the rush of the attacking enemy. Then someone ran or rode to the king his father, and asked for help, saying that his eldest son was in great danger; so he sent someone with twenty knights to aid the prince, who found him and his men leaning on their lances and swords on mounds of dead men, taking deep breaths and resting, awaiting a new onslaught of the enemy. So the fearful face of war was displayed, from the setting of the sun until the third quarter of the night, during which time the French raised a general war-cry three times and charged fifteen times, but nonetheless fled defeated.

The next day four battalions of fresh French troops came up, and as though nothing had happened to their companions, raised their war-cry for the fourth time and charged for the sixteenth time. The English, though weary from the previous day's fighting, resisted manfully, and after a great and bitter struggle put the enemy to flight, and pursued them; in the chase and from the beginning of the conflict, they killed three thousand men, that is on the Saturday and Sunday.

At noon on the Sunday, when the second battle was over, the king and the army moved a mile away from the dead and gave thanks to the Giver of victories and rested, taking a roll call of their men; only forty of the king's whole army were found to have been killed. That evening, having found the king of Bohemia's body, they had it washed in warm water, wrapped in clean linen and placed in a horse litter. The bishop of Durham and the clergy who were there celebrated the solemn rites for the dead in the presence of the king and his companions.

# ii. The prince's exploit at Calais, 1350

*The governor of Calais, Aimeric Pavia, a Lombard mercenary, has been approached by Geoffrey Charny, a leading French commander, and persuaded to betray Calais to the French for a large bribe. In case the plot misfires, Aimeric writes to Edward, giving him full details, so that he is in good standing with both sides.*

The king, however, anxious to keep the town, which he had won by no less an effort than a year's siege, hurriedly crossed the Channel, accompanied by his eldest son, the prince of Wales, Sir Roger Mortimer and a handful of others, and arrived only a few days before the date set for the plot. When he arrived in Calais, he prepared a crafty welcome for the French. Under the vaults inside the gateway of the portcullis and around the gates of the castle he stationed knights, building a thin wall in front of them, not cemented but made of dry stone and plastered level with the adjoining walls, and carefully faked to look like old work so that no-one would readily suspect that there were men in hiding there. Then he had the great beam of the drawbridge partly sawn through, yet left so that armed horsemen could ride over it. He also had a vaulted opening made in the tower above the bridge, and a large stone placed there; a trusted knight was put into hiding there, who was to break the sawn-through bridge at the right moment by throwing down the stone. The opening was then carefully closed over to the point where the man shut up inside could still count the enemy coming in, and the new work was blended in with the old. While all this was being done, only a few people knew of the presence of the king and prince of Wales, who had entered the town secretly.

On the day before the agreed date, Geoffrey Charny sent fifteen of his trusted men with a great part of the gold that was to be paid for the betrayal to check that Aimeric would keep his word and to explore the layout of the castle. They visited every turret and hidden corner, but saw nothing that caused them to change their plans. So the next day they raised the standard of the French king on the highest turret of the castle, and displayed the banners of Geoffrey and some other lords on the other turrets. The common soldiers of the garrison, who knew nothing of the plot, were so alarmed that, hurrying to arm themselves, they rushed to attack the castle. The French who had entered on the day before quickly captured Sir Thomas Kingston, who was also ignorant of the plot, and bound him with wooden fetters. Then some of them, sent out to their French lords who were in ambush outside the defences, displayed their standards and raised their banners, promising each other success provided they hurried to defend the castle against the common soldiers. So, sallying out of their hiding places with the usual and inbred pomp of the French race, a large number of French-men rushed in at the castle gates. The common soldiers could hardly be held back from attacking them, but their leaders withdrew them because of the danger of confusion in the planned ambush; and the king's comrades, who had been shut in their hiding places in the arches of the walls like hermits, hating the long delay of three days, prepared to attack. As soon as the man who had been walled up in the hole with a great stone saw that enough men had been admitted to be a match for his companions, he sent the great rock crashing down, which broke the drawbridge cutting off both entrance and exit for the enemy. The effect of the falling stone was backed up by the fall of the portcullis, which had been kept out of action at first and handed over to the French, in order to further their delusion of security. As the stone fell and broke the bridge, the hermit knights pushed down the back wall which hid them, forsook their religious solitude and challenged the French knights to battle. A fierce fight raged for a time, but the enemy were overcome and yielded to their conquerors.

As soon as the French who had remained outside realised that they had been tricked, they took to flight. The king, calling to him less than sixteen men at arms and the same number of archers (who knew nothing of his identity), attacked the fugitives, bringing down many of them, and performing dangerous feats in a very short space of time. However, the French realised that only a handful of men were following them, and eighty men at arms formed ranks against the king. I dare not say that it was wisdom or military prudence that led the king to pursue the enemy, but royal courage; but nonetheless he carried out this dangerous feat, and by the grace of God, came out of it with honour. When he saw that the French had re-formed, he threw away the sheath of his sword, and, encouraging his men and positioning them, he urged them to fight bravely. He posted the archers to one side of the men at arms on dry islands in the marsh, surrounded by muddy swamps so that the heavily armed horsemen and footsoldiers would be unable to reach them without sinking in the mire. The king encouraged his men and spoke to them courteously, saying 'Do your best, archers; I am Edward of Windsor.' Only then did the archers realise that the king was with them, and how necessary it would be to fight well; they bared their heads, arms and chests, and each one concentrated on not wasting a single arrow. They greeted the oncoming French bitterly enough, with a shower of sharp arrows. All the men at arms stood on a hard causeway, which was only broad enough for twenty men to march abreast; on either side lay the marsh, where armed men could not go and where the archers were safe, out of the way of their own men and showering the enemy with arrows from the flank. So the king and his men in the centre and the archers on each side killed and took prisoners, and put up a brave fight until the arrival of the prince of Wales put the French to flight.

After a long pursuit of the enemy, they returned to Calais and counted those who had fled and were captured; and they found that, according to the prisoners, a thousand knights and six hundred men at arms, and three thousand footsoldiers had come to take the castle. Of these Geoffrey de Charny and his son had been captured, beside many others.

1. Lead badge showing the prince adoring the trinity, within the Garter. Of unknown origin, its purpose is also mysterious: it may have been a cast from a mould used to make a badge in gold or silver, it may have decorated a bookbinding, or it may have been a funeral memento. It must date from c.1350-1376. (Trustees of the British Museum)

2. Edward III grants his son the principality of Aquitaine.
From a contemporary copy of the original deed (British
Library MS Cotton Nero D.vi, 31)

3. Original deed granting the principality of Aquitaine to Edward Prince of Wales (Public Record Office E30/1105)

4. Effigy of the Black Prince in Canterbury cathedral. An idealised representation, it is nonetheless consistent with other 'portraits' of the prince in illuminations of the late fourteenth century (National Monuments Record)

5. John II, a fourteenth-century portrait now in the Louvre
(Photo Giraudon, Paris)

6.  Pedro the Cruel: the contemporary funeral effigy now in the Museo Arquélogico Nacional Madrid.

7. The painting of the Trinity on the tester above the prince's tomb in Canterbury cathedral: a reconstruction drawn by Professor E. W. Tristram (Courtauld Institute of Art)

# 4. Campaign letters: the campaigns of 1355-6

## i. Introduction

This group of letters is less consistently propagandist in tone than those for the Crécy campaign, partly because there was less need to reassure those at home that the war was a worthwhile enterprise: public opinion was much more favourable than in 1346. Even so, a prudent retreat at the end of the 1355 expedition is made to look like a pursuit of the French forces in the region, whereas the prince was probably doing his best to get a weary army safely back home.

Sir John Wingfield was the prince's steward, and it is probably for this reason that he lays such stress on the economic benefits of the campaign: his practised eye assessed the damage done in money terms, and he even seeks confirmation of his estimates among captured local government papers: a very unromantic view of warfare! William Edendon, bishop of Winchester, to whom this and the prince's letter were addressed, was the head of the prince's council in England, but the letters are nonetheless public, and intended for circulation. That to Sir Richard Stafford is more intimate: Stafford had been sent back at the end of 1355 to obtain reinforcements, and this seems to have been a genuine private communication between two members of the prince's staff. Wingfield freely admits that he is uncertain of exactly what is happening, but takes pains to assure Stafford that his own men are safe and well. The last letter in the group is once more a public one: it is the fullest version of a letter sent by the prince to a number of towns and magnates in England announcing the victory at Poitiers, and was copied into the letter books of the City of London soon after its receipt.

## ii. Sir John Wingfield to the bishop of Winchester, 23 December (French)

My lord, as to news from these parts, you will be glad to know that my lord the prince and all the earls, barons, bannerets, knights and squires were in good health when this was written. And my lord has not lost any knights or squires on this expedition except for Sir John Lisle who was killed, very strangely, by a crossbow bolt on the third day after we entered enemy territory; and he died on 15 October. And, my lord, you will be glad to know that my lord has raided the county of Armagnac and taken several walled towns there, burning and destroying them, except for certain towns which he garrisoned. Then he went into the viscounty of Rivière, and took a good town called Plaisance, the chief town of the area, and burnt it and laid waste the surrounding countryside. Then he went into the county of Astarac, and took several towns and had them burnt and destroyed, and the countryside likewise, and took the chief town, called Samatan, which is as large as Norwich. Then he entered the county of Lisle and took some of the walled towns and had a number of good towns through which he passed burnt and destroyed. Then he entered the lordship of Toulouse, and we crossed the river Garonne and another a mile upstream of Toulouse, which is very large, because our enemy had broken all the bridges on both sides of Toulouse, except for the bridges in Toulouse, because the river goes through the town. The constable of France, the marshal of Clermont and the count of Armagnac were in the town at the time, with a great army. And the town of Toulouse is very large, strong and fine, and well fortified. And there was no-one in our army who knew where the ford was, but by God's grace we found it. And then he went through the lordship of Toulouse and took several good walled towns and burnt and destroyed them, laying waste the surrounding countryside. And then we entered the lordship of Carcassonne and took several good towns before we came to Carcassonne; and he took Carcassonne, which is larger, stronger and finer than York. And all that town and all the other towns in the region were burnt and destroyed. And then we marched for some days until we had crossed the Carcassonne region and entered the lordship of Narbonne: and we took several towns, and laid them waste, until we came to Narbonne. And the town of Narbonne resisted us and was taken by assault. The said town is only a little smaller than London, and is on the Mediterranean, from which it is only separated by about eight miles. And there is a harbour and landing place, and the river comes into Narbonne. And Narbonne is only sixty miles from Montpellier, seventy from Aigues-Mortes and a hundred and twenty from Avignon. You will be glad to know that the Holy Father sent his envoys to my lord, who were only thirty miles away from him. And the envoys sent a sergeant at arms, who was sergeant at arms at the pope's chamber door, with letters from them to my lord, asking for safe conduct to come to my lord, setting out their mission from the pope, which was to negotiate between my lord and his French adversaries. And the messenger was with the army for two days before my lord would see him or receive his letters. The reason was that my lord had news that the French army had come out of Toulouse towards Carcassonne, and my lord wanted to turn back on them suddenly; and so he did. And on the third day, when we should have attacked them, they had news of our movement before daybreak; and they retreated and disappeared towards the mountains and fastnesses, and returned towards Toulouse in long marches. The local people who acted as their guides when they went that way left them, and were captured as they returned home. And because the pope's sergeant of arms was in my custody, I made him question the guides who were captured; for the guide whom he questioned was the guide of the constable of France, a native of the country, and he could know and recognise that they were Frenchmen by questioning them. And I told the sergeant that he could go and report to the pope and the rest of them at Avignon what he had seen and heard. And as for my lord's reply to the envoys, you would be delighted to hear the whole story. For he refused to let the envoys come a step closer; but if they wanted to negotiate, they were to send to my lord the king, and my lord would do nothing except by the order of the king, nor would he listen to any proposals without his command. As to my lord's return in pursuit of his enemy, and the crossing of the Garonne, and the capture of castles and towns on the way, and the other things he did to the enemy as he pursued them, all of which was well and honourably done, as many know and Sir Richard Stafford and Sir William Burton will be able to explain more fully, I cannot describe in a letter, as it would take too long. My lord was in the field against his enemies for eight weeks and only took eleven rest days. It seems certain that since the war against the French king began, there has never been such destruction in a region as in this raid. For the countryside and towns which have been destroyed in this raid produced more revenue for the king of France in aid of his wars than half his kingdom; and that is without the profits of recoinage and the profits and customs which he takes from those of Poitou, as I could prove from authentic documents found in various towns in the tax-collectors' houses. For Carcassonne and Limoux, which is as large as Carcassonne, and two other towns near there, produce for the king of France each year the wages of a thousand men at arms and 100,000 old crowns towards the costs of the war. According to the records which we found, the towns around Toulouse, Carcassonne and Narbonne which we destroyed, together with Narbonne itself, produced each year, over and above this, 400,000 old crowns as war subsidies; and the citizens of the larger towns and other inhabitants, who should know about such matters, have told us this. And, by God's help, if my lord had money to continue this war and to profit the king and his honour, he could indeed enlarge the boundaries of his territory and take a number of places, because the enemy are in great disarray. In order to do this my lord has ordered all the earls and bannerets to stay in different places along the border in order to raid and damage the enemy's lands. My lord, that is all the news for the moment, but please write to me and let me know your wishes, and I will do my best to help. Most honoured lord, may God send you long life, joy and good health. Written at Bordeaux, Wednesday before Christmas.

## iii. Edward prince of Wales to the bishop of Winchester, 25 December. (French)

Reverend father in God and most trustworthy friend, as for news from these parts, this is to let you know that, since we last wrote to you, it was agreed by the advice and counsel of all the lords with us and the lords and barons of Gascony that we ought to march into

Armagnac, because the count of Armagnac was the leader of our
adversary's troops and his lieutenant in the whole of Languedoc,
and had done more damage to the liegemen of our most honoured
lord and father the king than anyone else in the region. So, in
pursuit of this, we marched through the country of Juliac, which
surrendered to us, as did the fortresses in it. Then we rode through
the country of Armagnac, laying waste the countryside, which
greatly encouraged the liegemen of our most honoured lord, whom
he had earlier attacked. From there we went into Astarac, and then
into Comminges, as far as a town called Samatan, the best town in
the region, whose inhabitants left it empty as our men approached.
Then we passed through the count of Isle's lands, until we came
within four miles of Toulouse, where the count of Armagnac and
other great men among the enemy were gathered. We stayed there
two days and then continued on our march, crossing in one day
the two rivers of Garonne and Ariège, four miles upstream from
Toulouse, which are difficult enough to cross, with hardly any loss
of men; and we encamped for the night about four miles beyond
Toulouse. And we marched through the country round Toulouse
where many good towns and fortresses were burnt and destroyed,
because the region is very rich and fertile; and not a day passed
without a town, castle, or fortress being taken by one or other
of our battalions or by all of them. We continued to Avignonet, a
large and strong town which we took by assault: all our battalions
encamped in the town. Then we went to Castelnaudary, which we
reached on All Saints' Eve [October 31] and remained there for the
feast day, the entire army encamped inside the town. From there we
marched to Carcassonne, a fine large town, held by important
commanders, with numerous men at arms and common soldiers;
the majority of the inhabitants of the country around Toulouse had
fled there, but when we arrived they abandoned the town and
retreated into the old town, a very strong castle. We stayed there
two days, the whole army being inside the town, and spent the
whole of the third day burning the town, so that it was completely
destroyed. Then we rode right through the region round Carcassonne until we came to Narbonne, a noble town, and larger than
Carcassonne. The inhabitants abandoned the town and took refuge
in the castle, where the viscount of Narbonne was, with a garrison

of 500 men at arms, or so it was said. We stayed there two days; once again the whole army stayed in the town. Then the pope sent two bishops to us, who sent for safe-conducts to us, which we did not grant them. For we did not want to enter into any treaty until we knew the wishes of our most honoured lord and father the king, particularly since we had news that he had crossed into France with an army. So we sent letters back to them saying that if they wanted to negotiate, they should go to him, and we would do whatever he commanded; and so they went back. Then we held a council as to where it would be best to march next; and because we had news from prisoners and others that our enemy had gathered and was coming after us to give battle, we turned back towards them and expected a battle within the next three days. And when we turned back, they retreated to Toulouse. So we pursued them, making long marches to Toulouse: and then we crossed the Garonne at Carbonne twelve miles from Toulouse, where we rested for that day and the following night. Before midnight news came that the whole enemy army under the count d'Armagnac, the constable of France, marshal Clermont and the prince of Orange and other noblemen of the region had come out of Toulouse and were encamped about eight miles from our rearguard, having lost some of their men and carts as they encamped. At this we marched towards them, sending on Bartholomew Burghersh, John Chandos, James Audley, Baldwin Botetourt and Thomas Felton and others, about thirty in all, to get definite information about the enemy. They rode on towards the enemy until they came to a town where they found 200 of the latter's men at arms, with whom they fought and captured thirty-five of them. This made the enemy retreat in great fear to their camp, and they marched to the towns of Lombez and Sauveterre, which are only two miles apart. We encamped outside the towns that same night, so close that we could see their campfires. But there was between us a very large deep river, and that night, before we came, they had broken the bridges, so that we could only cross the next day after we had got our men to repair the bridges. From there the enemy moved to the town of Gimont, which we reached on the same day as them, and before they could enter the town our men captured or killed many of them. That same night we encamped outside the town, and waited there the whole of the next day, hoping that a battle might take place. And the same [next] day we and the whole army were in battle order before sunrise, when news came that before daybreak most of the enemy had left; only the commanders remained in the town, which was large and strong and could have been held against large numbers of men. So we returned to our quarters and had a council as to what to do. It was clear that the enemy did not want a battle, so it was agreed that we should return towards our own lands. Sir Richard Stafford will tell you about this more fully than we can in a letter; please give full credence to everything he has to say and to show to you. Revered father in God and most trustworthy friend, may the Almighty keep you always. Written under our privy seal at Bordeaux, Christmas day.

## iv. Sir John Wingfield to Sir Richard Stafford, 22 January. (French)

Most dear lord and most trustworthy friend, as for news since you left, this is to tell you that five fortified towns have surrendered, namely Port Ste Marie, Clairac, Tonneins, Bourg St Pierre, Castelsagrat and Brassac, and seventeen castles, that is, Quiller, Buzet, Lavaignac, two castles called Boulogne which are very close to each other, Montjoie, Virech, Fresquenet, Montendre, Pusdechales, Montpon, Montagnac, Vauclair, Benevent, Listrac, Plassac, Crudestablison and Montreal. Sir John Chandos, Sir James Audley and your men who are with them, and the other Gascons in their company, Sir Baldwin Botetourt and his company, and Sir Reginald Cobham took the town called Castelsagrat by assault, and the bastard de Lisle, who was captain of the town was killed as they attacked by an arrow which went through his head. Sir Reginald has turned back towards Lanedac and Sir Baldwin towards Brassac, with their troops; and Sir John and Sir James with their men have stayed at Castelsagrat, and have enough of all kinds of supplies to last until midsummer, except only for fresh fish and greens, according to their letters. So you need not worry about your own men. There are more than three hundred armed men in the town, three hundred foot soldiers and a hundred and fifty archers. And they have raided towards Agen, burning and destroying all their mills, and have burnt and broken all the bridges across the Garonne, and taken a castle outside the town and garrisoned it. Sir John d'Armagnac and the seneschal of Agenais, who were in the town of Agen, did not once poke their heads out, nor did any of their men; yet our people have been outside the town twice. Sir Boucicaut has come, as has Sir Arnaut d'Espaigne and Grismouton de Chambly, with three hundred lances and three hundred Lombard footsoldiers; they are at Moissac in Quercy, only a few miles from Castelsagrat and Brassac. There will be a good company there for each to try his comrade's worth. Sir Bartholomew is at Cognac with 120 men at arms from the prince's household and 120 archers, and the captal de Buch, the lord of Montferrand and the lord of Curton are with him, with 300 lances and 120 archers and 200 footsoldiers, and there are men at arms at Taillebourg, Tonnay and Rochefort, probably about six hundred lances in all. At the moment they are out on a raid towards Anjou and Poitou. The earls of Suffolk, Oxford and Salisbury, the lord of Mussidan, Elie de Pommiers and other Gascons with more than 500 lances, 200 footsoldiers and 300 archers are at the moment in the area of Rocamadour; they have been away for twelve days and had not returned when this letter was sent. Sir John Chandos, Sir James and Sir Baldwin and the men in their company are also out on a raid in their region. Sir Reginald and the men of the prince's household and the Gascons who are with them are also out on a raid. The earl of Warwick has been at Tonneins and at Clairac and has taken these towns; at the moment he is somewhere near Marmande, trying to destroy the enemy's provisions and other things. My lord (the prince) is at Libourne and the lord of Pommiers at Fronsac, a mile or two from Libourne. The prince's men are at St Emilion and Libourne, and Berard d'Albret is with them. The prince is awaiting news which he expects to receive, and is going to decide what his best course of action is once he has heard the news. At the moment the count of Armagnac is at Avignon, as is the king of Aragon. As to the other reports about different places, which you know about, I have no further information at the time of writing. Most dear lord, that is all I have to tell you; but please remember to send news to the prince as soon as you possibly can. Written at Libourne, 22 January.

## v. Edward prince of Wales to the mayor, aldermen and commons of London, 22 October. (French)

Most dear and well beloved, as to news from the parts where we are, this is to let you know that since we sent word to our most respected lord and father the king that we were intending to ride towards our enemy in France, we made our way through Périgord and Limousin directly to Bourges where we expected to find the king's son, the count of Poitiers. The chief reason for our going there was that we expected to hear that the king had crossed, but since we did not find either the count or a great army there, we moved towards the Loire, and sent our men to see if we could cross it. They met the enemy and fought them, killing some of them and taking the rest prisoner. The prisoners said that the French king had sent Grismouton, who was in their company, to discover news of us and our army; and the king had also sent the lord of Craon, Sir Boucicaut, the marshal of Clermont and others in a different direction for the same reason. The prisoners said that the king had made up his mind to fight us when we were on our way to Tours, and that he was drawing near to Orleans. The next day news came to our camp that the said lords of Craon and Boucicaut were in a castle very near our camp: so we decided to go there, and took up positions around them. We decided to attack the place, and it was taken by force, many of their men being taken or killed, and some of our people being killed. But the lords of Craon and Boucicaut withdrew into a strong tower there, which held out for five days before we took it. Then they surrendered, and we learnt that all the bridges over the Loire were broken down, and that there was nowhere for us to cross. At which we went straight to Tours, and spent four days before the town: the count of Anjou and the marshal of Clermont were there with a great number of men. When we left we made our way across several dangerous rivers, intending to meet our dear cousin the duke of Lancaster, of whom we heard for certain that he was trying to march towards us. At this time cardinal Périgord came to us at Montbazon, nine miles from Tours, where he talked at length about a truce or peace; and we answered his speech by telling him that peace could not be made, nor would we involve ourselves in negotiations, without orders from our very dear lord and father the king. Nor did we think that it would be advisable for us to agree to a truce, because we were told while we were there that the king was hastening to fight us. So we went towards Châtellerault, where there was a crossing over the river Vienne and stayed there for four days to find out for certain what the king was doing. He came with his army to Chauvigny, twenty miles from us, to cross the same river towards Poitiers, and on hearing this we decided to hasten towards him on the road which he would have to take in order to fight him. But his battalions had already passed when we got to the place where we expected to meet him, and only part of his army, some seven hundred men at arms, fought us. We captured the counts of Auxerre and Joigny and the lord of Castillon and many others were taken or killed on both sides; and our men pursued them for twelve miles, as far as Chauvigny. So we had to encamp there to reassemble our troops; and the next day we went straight in the direction of the king. We sent out scouts who found him and his army ready for battle in the fields about four miles from Poitiers, and we approached him as closely as possible in order to take up positions. On foot ourselves, we put the army into battle order, ready to fight him, when the said cardinal arrived, begging for a brief delay so that men could be chosen from both sides to discuss a peace agreement, and he undertook to see that this would be done. We took council, and granted his request, and delegations were sent from each side to negotiate, but nothing came of it. Then the cardinal asked for a truce at his pleasure to prevent the battle, which we refused. The French asked that chosen knights from each side should agree on a place where the battle was to be fought, so that the battle would be sure to take place. So matters were put off for that day, and the armies on both sides remained in position all night until early the next morning. There were some troops between the main armies, but even they refused to yield any advantage by being the first to attack. Because we were short of supplies and for other reasons, it was agreed that we should take a path traversing their front, so that if they wanted to attack or to approach us in a position which was not in any way greatly to our disadvantage we would give battle. This was done and the battle took place the day before the eve of St Matthew (21 September). Praise be to God, the enemy were defeated, and the king, his son and many other nobles taken or killed, as our very dear and beloved knight Neil Loring, our chamberlain, who is bringing this, will tell you in more detail from his own knowledge, as we cannot write it all down. Please give him full credence and trust. May Our Lord keep you. Given under our privy seal at Bordeaux, 22 October.

# 5. Geoffrey le Baker: Chronicle

Geoffrey le Baker's account of the 1355 campaign is based on a campaign diary very similar to *The acts of war of Edward III*. It stands apart from the rest of his chronicle in its relatively terse narration of events, and he in fact begins his outline of the 'great raid' by a summary of its results. He continues, 'Besides, in order to make these matters clearer, it will be of interest to put in the individual day's marches of the prince in Narbonnese France.' However, he does not quote his original directly, but rewrites it. It is nonetheless the most valuable version of the prince's exploits in the south-west, giving considerably more detail than either of the campaign letters.

When it comes to the battle of Poitiers, le Baker is writing in a rather different style. A very brief campaign diary survives in the Malmesbury chronicle, but Baker does not use this, giving a fairly general account of the prince's march to the Loire. He then begins to give more detail: the failure to burn Tours because of storms is confirmed exactly by local French sources, and although he is less than specific about the movements before the battle itself, his account of the actual fighting does represent an eyewitness version, set down within at most four years of the battle, and possibly only a few months afterwards. Who his informant was we do not know: but there are indications that he must have been with the prince of Wales for at least part of the battle, since Baker specifically tells us what the prince could and could not see in relation to French movements. The only doubtful point is at the opening of the battle, when the prince is said to have moved across a stream, in terms which can only describe the river Miosson, towards the French. Now other sources make it clear that the prince attempted a retreat just before the fighting began, and the earl of Warwick's division crossed the Miosson heading south, only to recross it when the French attacked. A possible explanation is that Baker's informant was with Warwick's division, which later merged with that of the prince: his description of the archers' movements in the valley is much more precise than his knowledge of the rearguard's part in the fighting, which would probably have been visible from the prince's position.

Baker has added to this eyewitness version his own rhetoric, which is almost impossible to transmute into acceptable modern terms; the reader will have to bear with the scenes of blood and gore, which are unpleasant enough in the original but seem even cruder in plain English. He also invents two speeches made by the prince; I have given Stow's Elizabethan translation of that to the archers, which belongs not to history, but to a literary tradition going back to Livy.

# i. The prince's campaign in south-west France, 1355

On the first Sunday of the month, 4 October, divine service was celebrated, and on the Monday following the prince set out from Bordeaux against the enemy, staying that night two miles from Bordeaux at the castle of Ornon. The next day the army followed a narrow road through woods, through the middle of the walled town of Longon; it was a long march, on which many horses were lost, ending at the castle of Castets-en-Dorthe. On the Thursday they reached the city of Bazas, which has a cathedral and a Minorite convent. There, on the Friday, a proclamation was issued throughout the army that everyone was to bear the arms of St George; rumour had it that the enemy were doing the same. On Saturday, the army reached Castelnau, where three castles belonging to three different lords can be seen from a long way off. On the Sunday, the 11th of the month, the army crossed the Bordeaux Landes which belong to the count of Foix. This was a long day's march through deserted and difficult country, and many horses were lost. That day, in the desert called the Landes, two miles from Arouille, the standards were unfurled and the army was divided into battalions. In command of the first, consisting of three thousand men at arms, were the earl of Warwick, who was constable, Reginald Cobham (the marshal), Lord Beauchamp of Somerset, Lord Clifford, Sir Thomas Hampton (the standard-bearer) and seven Gascon barons. In the middle battalion, containing seven thousand men at arms apart from clerks and foot-soldiers, were the prince, with a double standard, the earl of Oxford, Sir Bartholomew Burghersh, Sir John Lisle, Lord Wilby, Lord de la

Ware, Sir Maurice Berkeley (son of Sir Thomas, who was still alive but elderly), Sir John Bourchier, Sir John Roos (mayor of Bordeaux), the captal de Buch, the lord of Caumont and the lord of Montferrand as standard-bearer. In the last battalion were another four thousand men at arms under the earls of Suffolk and Salisbury and the lord of Pommiers, who led a contingent from Béarn. In the whole army there were, including men at arms, clerks, footsoldiers, archers, Welshmen and others, over 60,000 men. And that day Jankin Berefort and others were knighted; and the town of Arouille, with three other towns, whose commander was Guillaume Raymond, an ally of the English, were surrendered again to the prince. The army lodged in these towns, and spent two days there. Those who wished to do so went out and took provisions and forage, burning enemy territory, and doing everything that would bring back the country to the king's peace. On the Tuesday, after the army encamped at Monclar, the castle was surrendered; from this day onwards the prince went out into the fields and spent the night in tents, because of a fire which broke out in the town and burnt it: he did this both to avoid disturbances at night and to be ready for the enemy. That day, after three towns had been entered and burnt, William Stratton★ and some others were knighted. Besides this Sir John Lisle was wounded by a crossbow bolt at the fortress of Estang, and died the following day, much to the grief of the army. On Wednesday and Thursday the army halted, and on Friday they encamped outside the stronghold of Nogaro. On Saturday they came to Plaisance, a fine, strong town: all the inhabitants fled, and the count of Montlezun with many knights and squires was captured in the castle by the captal de Buch, the lord of Montferrand and Adam de Louches, newly knighted that day. On the third Sunday, St Luke's day, they halted; the fortress of Galiax was taken by assault and burnt. On the Monday, having set fire to Plaisance, they left the town of Beaumarchez to the right and lodged at a town belonging to the archbishop of Auch, called Bassoues; on that day Sir Richard Stafford, the earl of Stafford's brother, raised his standard for the first time. On the Tuesday, the said town was surrendered, but because it belonged to the church, the prince did not allow anyone to enter it, except certain people commissioned to obtain

★ Stratton was the prince's tailor for many years.

supplies. On Wednesday, they left the fine town of Montesquiou to the left and came to the noble town of Mirande, belonging to the count of Comminges, full of men at arms; and the prince stayed in the great Cistercian monastery at Berdoues, where no living thing was found. On the Thursday, they halted; no damage was done to the monastery. On Friday, they left the noble, fine and rich country of Armagnac and entered the country called Astarac; here the roads were difficult, hard and mountainous. They lodged at Seissan, which, despite strict orders from the prince to the contrary, was burnt. That day and for the three following days, the way lay near the high mountains of Aragon (i.e. the Pyrenees). On Saturday they came to Simorre, where the rearguard lodged in a great monastery abandoned by the Dominicans; the centre was at Villefranche and the rearguard at Tournau, all wealthy towns and full of supplies, but abandoned by their fleeing inhabitants. On the fourth Sunday, St Crispin and Crispinian's day, they crossed a ford in the lands of the count of Comminges, which reached as far as Toulouse; but they had been laid waste by fire and sword. And then they left a town called Sauveterre in Astarac to the left, and passed a strong town called Lombez, where Pope John XXII was ordained bishop; and they lodged in a large and rich town called Samatan, where there was a Minorite convent; but it was burnt along with the town. On the Monday, they went through fertile, level and beautiful country to the town of St Foi and then to St Lys. On the Tuesday they rested; and on the Wednesday, the feast of Sts Simon and Jude, the army crossed the river Gironde, swift, rocky and very frightening; and on the same day they also crossed the Ariège, even more dangerous than the Gironde, and went downstream to Toulouse. No horse had ever previously crossed these rivers; which put the people of the region into a state of terror, not knowing what to do and unable to flee, because they had believed that they were safe because of the rivers. Nor did they know how to fight back, since they had never been involved in warfare before. That night the prince lodged at La Croix Falgarde, a little town a mile from Toulouse. After this our men hardly rode for a single day without taking by assault towns, fortresses and castles, which they sacked and burnt. On Thursday, they reached the large and fine town of Mongiscard, part of the inheritance of Aimery de la Fossade, confiscated by the

French usurper because he remained loyal to the English king. Near the town were twelve windmills, which were all set on fire. There two spies or scouts were captured, who said that the count of Armagnac was at Toulouse, and the constable of France at Montauban, twelve miles from Toulouse, expecting the arrival of the army to besiege Toulouse. On Friday, the army took the straight king's highway towards Avignonet, via Baziège and Villefranche; the whole army lodged in the large town called Avignonet, which belonged to the French usurper. The centre and rearguard were in one suburb, the vanguard in another part of the suburb, and the Gascons and Béarnese in the town itself, all of whose inhabitants had fled. Twenty windmills were burnt there. On the Saturday, 31 October, they lodged in a large town called Castelnaudary, where the church of St Michael, belonging to secular canons, and the convents of the Minorites and Carmelites, as well as the hospital of St Antony and a town called Le Mas Saintes Puelles, with an Augustine convent, were all burnt. On the Sunday, All Saints Day, the army rested; some of the men left it and took a town, whose inhabitants paid 10,000 florins to be spared with their goods. On Monday they went past St Martin Lalande, and a large town called Villepinte, entering the lands of Carcassonne; the prince lodged at a village called Alzonne. On Tuesday they came to Carcassonne, a beautiful, extremely wealthy and well built town, larger inside its walls than London. Between the Bourg and the city, which is surrounded by a double wall, a river runs under a fine stone bridge, with a fine hospital at the foot of the bridge. In the town there were four convents of the four orders of friars; the friars did not flee, but the townspeople and Poor Clares who also lived there fled to the city. The whole army was lodged in comfort in the Bourg, and hardly occupied three-quarters of it; there was an abundance of muscat wine and of both delicacies and ordinary provisions. That day the army was drawn up in good order outside the town, and the sons of the lord of Albret and lord Basset of Drayton were knighted, who at once rode out with his own banner raised. Roland Daneys* and others were also knighted. On Wednesday and Thursday the army rested in the town; a truce was arranged, and envoys were sent to arrange a peace treaty with those in the city. The citizens offered

* He had served the prince in his household for at least ten years.

250,000 gold écus if the Bourg was spared from the flames. The prince answered, when offered the gold, that he did not come for gold but for justice, not to sell but to take cities. Since the citizens continued to fear the French usurper, did not wish to obey their natural lord, or indeed did not dare to because they expected the usurper to take his revenge, the prince therefore ordered the town to be burnt, but the religious houses were to be spared. On Friday, the Bourg was set on fire, and the army left; and he heard later from friars and others that it was burnt to ashes. That day, St Leonard's day, the roads were difficult, rocky and crossed by rivers; the army left the castle of Bouillonac to the left, and crossed the country and towns called Rustiques, burning the whole area. Saturday's journey was wearisome, and the army was afflicted by wind and dust; they passed on the left a freshwater lake, sixty miles in circumference, called Esebon, into and out of which no water flowed, except by rain or evaporation. They came to a town called Lézignan, which was surrendered to the prince but was left untouched because of Isido de Bretagne, a friend of the prince, to whom it belonged; the prince lodged at a good town called Canet. On Sunday, 8 November, they crossed the Aude, partly by a ford called Château de Terre, and partly by a new but incomplete bridge. The rest of the day's march was through steep hills, and they reached the large city of Narbonne, from which the country called Narbonnese France gets its name. This is a strong, well walled city with a large church (the cathedral of St Justin), a fine bishop's castle, and an extremely strong tower for the viscount of the town. It also has a suburb called the Bourg, larger and better built than that of Carcassonne. In the Bourg were four convents of the Mendicant orders. Between the spacious and wealthy Bourg and the very well-walled city, runs the river Aude, coming from Carcassonne and flowing into the Mediterranean, which is six miles from Narbonne. Between the city and the Bourg are two stone bridges, and a third of wood, with another of stone for the merchants' baggage carts, very well built. The prince lodged in the house of the Carmelite friars; but throughout the night and all the following day the citizens and the army fired catapults and other machines at each other; many on both sides were wounded, but no-one was killed. On the Tuesday, the Bourg was set on fire by flaming crossbow bolts, and the army moved to the edge of the river, crossing it in a number of places. During the crossing the townsmen broke up two of the prince's carts and plundered them, doing much damage. The prince lodged at the town and castle of Aubian. On Wednesday, St Martin's day, the march was long and difficult, particularly bad for horses because it was rocky and there was no water or other supplies; the horses had to drink wine instead of water, and the food was cooked in wine, because no other liquid except wine or oil was to be had. On Thursday Theodoric van Dale, usher of the prince's chamber, was knighted; and they passed a good town called Homps, where the staff of the count of Armagnac had stayed the previous night; the centre lodged at Azille, a good town belonging to the count of Isle. The prince spent the night at the Minorite house, where a great quantity of muscat wine, kept in the cellars for the countess of Isle, was wasted. On the same day the town of Pépieux, and the castle there called Laredorte, were destroyed; captured enemy scouts reported that the constable of France and the count of Armagnac had intended to spend the night in the towns where the army had spent the night. On Friday the army lodged at Villemagne, a poor place with few houses and little water, after a long and waterless march. On Saturday they turned back towards Gascony, leaving to the right the lake of Esebon and Carcassonne and the whole of the previous journey, and the rear-guard lodged at a good town called St Hilaire and the centre at Pennautier, where a fortified tower was captured; but the prince lay beyond the bridge on a pleasant riverbank. From there the country-side on both sides was burnt, including Pezens, where the vanguard had lodged. On Sunday, St Machutus' day, they entered fair open country, and made a long march, the army pressing on because the prince was to lodge at the great abbey of the Blessed Virgin at Prouille, where, in separate cloisters, a hundred friars, preachers and 140 women recluses called Preacheresses, live off their estates; and here the prince, with many others, was devoutly admitted to the spiritual brotherhood of the house. That day the army burnt among others the town of Limoux, where there was a friars' convent, greater than that of Carcassonne, and a fine town called Fanjeaux, which had twenty-one windmills, and the towns of Villar and Lasserre. On Monday the centre lodged at a good town called Belpech, which, after a long defence, was taken by assault. The castle also surrendered, but the prince gave orders that they were not to be burnt, because they belonged to the lordship of the count of Foix. On the Tuesday morning, the river Hers was crossed, in small groups; they entered a fairly desolate country, but about mid-day they came to a great Cistercian monastery, founded by an ancestor of the count of Foix, called Boulbonne. Here the prince was met with great rejoicing by the said count, the greatest magnate in all Aquitaine; he had escaped from the French usurper's prison in Paris, in which he had been imprisoned for two years; and from then on he remained faithful to the prince. The count was then young, about twenty-one, and not yet knighted. That day they rode through the count's lordship to Mazères and Calmon, which are separated by a river. On the far bank is a ruined castle. They left the large town of Cintegabelle on the right and a powerful castle called Auterive, belonging to the French. But nothing was burnt that day out of respect for the said count and his neighbours. Then they crossed the dangerous river Ariège, as they had done previously on the feast of Sts Simon and Jude. Toulouse, which they had previously passed a mile to the left, was now left unharmed twelve miles to the right; and the centre lodged in the large town of Miremont, which was burnt together with its castle. On Wednesday, they passed a castle belonging to the count of Foix called Montaut, at the foot of which the cavalry crossed the wide river Garonne in single file, to the astonishment of the country people. Throughout the year boats are kept here for people to cross, but these had been removed by men from Noe in order to hold up the army. When, by God's grace, they had crossed the Garonne, according to men captured afterwards in enemy castles, no-one was able to cross because of floods caused by days of rain, so that their crossing was justly ascribed to the hand of God. Noe was taken by assault, and the castle surrendered; the rearguard spent the night in the latter. They left the Garonne to the left, and came to the town of Marquefave, which was captured by a miracle. Then the centre crossed the said river yet again, to the amazement of the country-men, to the strong town of Carbonne, defended by a wall on one side and the river on the other. It was taken by assault before the prince arrived, so that the victors were able to lodge there; the prince, as was his invariable custom, encamped outside. On Thursday, in calm and delightful weather, the army rested, taking its ease after the continuous hard work of the previous days. On Friday, learning that the French were nearby, grouped in five large battalions, our men left their encampment and drew themselves up in battle order about a mile away. When the army was drawn up, someone hallooed at a hare; the enemy heard this and sent forty lances, who retreated in haste as soon as they saw the army drawn up in order, and the whole enemy army fled in confusion, so prisoners taken during the pursuit reported. That day Bartholomew Burghersh, John Chandos and James Audley, at the head of eighty lances, set out on a scouting mission and, reaching the tail of the French army, they captured thirty-two knights and squires, among them the lord of Romery; they also killed many carters and destroyed the enemy's provisions. In the evening the prince lodged at Mauvesin, and four French men at arms, taking refuge in the church there from the English, only lost their horses and armour. The Saturday was rainy, and they took a narrow, bad road to the castle of Aurade, whence the prince spent the night; it was burnt the next day. On Sunday, St Cecilia's day, having made a long march, they realised that the enemy were on the other side of a large hill, near and below the town of Gimont, so that the English, delayed until midnight, sent in the meanwhile sixty lances with some archers to the right, to the town of Aurimont, where they found 400 men at arms of the constable of France's company, and forced them to abandon the town, killing and capturing some of them as they pursued them towards Gimont. So the centre lodged, none too well, at Aurimont, the vanguard at Celimont, a little town only a mile away from the enemy. The next day, St Clement's day, the carters and officials were ordered to stay at Aurimont; the fighting men were drawn up in order and awaited the enemy in the open field, but in vain. The prince, indeed, sent out scouts to Gimont, only to find that the enemy had fled about midnight, so that they were technically defeated, especially since they fled from their adversary (the English) out of sheer terror, when the latter had sought them for a long while, after long and bad marches, and had several times found them nearby. On Tuesday, after a long day, the army camped in the open fields, where, for lack of water, they gave the horses wine to drink; the following day they were drunk, and

could not keep a steady footing, with the result that many horses
were lost. On St Catherine's day, a river was crossed, the army
dispersing over a wide area; it was hoped to meet the enemy. Leaving the walled town of Fleurance (formerly English) to the right,
they passed the large town of Ste Radegonde; and the centre lodged
at the town of Réjaumont, taken by storm and therefore burnt. On
Thursday they rested, and a stray man at arms who was captured
reported that a quarrel of no small proportions had arisen between
the constable of France and the count of Armagnac, because the
count had promised to fight a battle on their behalf, but had done
nothing, running away shamefully several times, and the count was
blamed for this. On the Friday they crossed a large river in scattered
groups, and marched for the rest of the day between walled towns
and strong castles; the centre lodged at Lasserre. The duke of Lancaster had laid waste this town, some three miles from the good
town of Condom, and had destroyed its castle, razing it to the
ground. On Saturday, crossing a river in scattered groups, they
entered a narrow forest road, where many of the Gascons and all the
Béarnese were given leave to return home; and the army encamped
at a good strong town, with which we were at peace – it had always
been English – called Mézin. On this day the standards were furled,
and the prince finished his journey in peace. On Sunday, St Andrew's
eve, the prince rested, receiving the homage and oaths of loyalty of
the townsmen. On the second day, the feast-day of the apostle, they
came after a long march to Casteljaloux, where there are three
castles, one built in the marshes. On the Tuesday, the prince lodged
at the castle of Meulan, three miles from Casteljaloux, and many of
his household crossed desolate wooded country near the Cistercian
monastery of Montepouillon and through the forest belonging to
the English king called Boismajeur, to the town of La Réole, which
the earl of Derby had captured in the past; the castle was surrendered within eight weeks of the capture of the town. On the
Wednesday, the prince came to La Réole, his horses and earls crossing the Gironde in a place where none could remember a horse
crossing before. At La Réole, the prince held a council, at which it
was ordered that the magnates and barons should spend the winter
at different places on the border, to protect Gascon lands from the
inroads of the French; and they did many excellent deeds, often

sallying out from the places assigned to them, leaving a suitable guard. They seized considerable wealth from enemy lands, upholding youthful feats of arms and enriching their own country; but I cannot deal with all their exploits without writing at great length.

## ii. The prince's campaign of 1356

So, gathering the forces which he had with him in the duchy, intending to cross France and meet his father, he came to Bergerac, whence he was told that the count of Armagnac intended to ravage the country after he had gone, and had prepared a considerable army to do this. He therefore sent back to guard his lands the seneschal of Gascony, and Sir Berard d'Albret, as well as the mayor of Bordeaux and other Gascons and a large number of knights.

From there the prince made his way into France, through the counties of Limousin and Berry. Following the good custom of his predecessors the prince urged those who were about to set out with him against the enemy not to wander about unarmed, but to arm their bodies with bodily armour and their souls with penitence and the sacrament of the Eucharist, so that they would be ready to fight those who had rebelled against his father, living in worldly honour and dying in eternal honour, and with God and with men carrying off the victory. Nor did he fail in the skills of a wise commander; but he appointed the distinguished knights John Chandos, James Audley and their companions, all skilled in warfare, to act as scouts in the enemy countryside lest they laid ambushes in woods for our men. He himself took charge of the camp, seeing that it was moved each day when the road had been inspected and provided with defences against night attacks. He also saw that the usual watch was kept, and went round them himself with his more valiant comrades, each part of the army being visited in case something out of order exposed it to danger. When they entered Poitou, the scouts reported that the usurper had assembled a large army at Orléans, and knew of the prince's approach, as events showed. Indeed, he sent out a knight called Grismouton de Chambly to find out where our army was, at the head of two hundred men at arms. Our scouts engaged him and captured thirty of his knights and footsoldiers and many others killed, so that none of them could go back and inform the main army what had become of his companions. With this initial success to encourage them, our army moved to Romorantin, where they found the lords of Craon and Boucicaut, sent out on a scouting mission. They occupied the town so quickly that, having killed many of the enemy, they forced the leaders to take refuge in the castle. After taking up lodgings in the town, the prince ordered an attempt to be made to take the castle by assault the next day. The following day our men at arms crossed the moat and attacked the castle walls, which they hastened to scale with ladders, while others burnt down doors; they forced their way in and killed many knights, while the two lords retreated with a number of others into the keep. At this the prince ordered his council to gather, to decide whether to leave those in the tower alone or to compel them to surrender by a siege. Because it was reported that the French usurper was not more than thirty miles away, the council judged it better not to move and to await the usurper with a view to battle, rather to seek to avoid it, because they were very anxious to come to grips with him and reckoned that if they began a siege it would provoke the French into trying to raise. In the end, it was decided not to retire from the castle until those shut up in it were either captured or surrendered themselves, unless a major battle was expected. The prince gave orders that stone-throwing machines and tortoises for the protection of the miners should be built. The machines, manned by specially trained troops, destroyed the roof of the tower and the battlements with round stones. They also set fire to the tunnel which the miners had dug and which reached to the foundations of the castle, burning the timbers which had hardly been strong enough to prevent the foundations from collapsing on the men who were digging it, and these would have fallen into the mine. But the helpless besieged saw their safety threatened by so many dangers that they begged to be allowed to surrender; and this was agreed in accordance with the prince's wishes on the sixth day of the siege.

After this scouts came in bringing word that the French usurper was moving down to Tours in order to form his army into battle order. So the prince, eager for battle because peace usually accompanies it, led his army towards the camp of the usurper, hoping to find a new ford across the Loire, as he had done earlier on the Garonne.

But heavy rains had made the Loire a raging torrent, and it was impossible for our men to ford it; to make matters more difficult, the usurper had had all the bridges between Blois and Tours, between which the Loire flows, broken down, so that there should be no road open between the prince and the duke of Lancaster, who could easily see each other's camp fires at night. The prince followed the course of the Loire eastwards and encamped near Tours, where he waited for four days, hoping that the usurper, who was three miles away would give battle. Here Bartholomew Burghersh and others were told to burn the suburbs of Tours; but the weather, which had been fine and calm since the beginning of the journey, now broke, and it rained and thundered for three days, so that, thanks to St Martin, patron saint of Tours, its enemies were unable to burn the town. The prince now learnt that the usurper had waited thirty miles away at Blois but had now crossed the Loire by a bridge situated between two very strong castles and was heading for Poitou.

When he learnt that the usurper had avoided battle, the prince hastened to block his path, but he failed to do this. However, he took a route which he thought would be the quickest, across three rivers, and attacked the rear of the enemy army, capturing two counts, those of Joigny and Auxerre, and the marshal of Burgundy. These were held to ransom, but a large number of men at arms were killed in the skirmish. As night approached, our men rested in a forest; and the next day continued towards Poitou. Our scouts discovered that the usurper had drawn up his men in battle order; and soon afterwards other scouts came in with reports that he was moving in our direction, and advised the prince to choose a place for battle and draw up his troops in case the enemy caught us unawares. The prince and everyone with him at once dismounted, handing their chargers and horses to their squires, to be kept in reserve for pursuing the enemy. A few knights rode up and down between the armies, ready for the customary skirmishes and single combats. The vanguard of our army was under the command of the earls of Warwick and Oxford; the prince led the centre; and the rearguard was given to the earls of Salisbury and Suffolk. In the whole of the prince's army there were exactly four thousand men-at-arms, a thousand sergeants and two thousand archers.

The French nobles approached in their full pomp and glory, dismissing the English as a mere handful, because their host contained eight thousand knights, not counting men at arms, under eighty-seven standards. Many of our men complained because a great part of the army that had originally been gathered had been sent to defend Gascony. There was with the French a Scotsman, William Douglas, a powerful man in Scotland, who had seen much campaigning in the Scottish wars. The usurper had knighted him again, because he knew that he had been a ferocious adversary of the English and had fought against them several times, he freely listened to his advice, and placed great trust in him. William led two hundred Scottish men at arms, whom he had brought from his own country. They were well aware that throughout the wars of the present king of England the English were mostly accustomed to fighting on foot, imitating the Scots, ever since Stirling. So William preferred to follow his nation's style of fighting and attack on foot rather than on horseback, and he persuaded the usurper and the rest of the French to fight in similar fashion. The unlawful usurper, foolishly agreeing to the counsel of this busybody, sent his warhorses back to the city (Poitiers) lest anyone should use them to take flight, only retaining five hundred horses clad in armour to protect them from arrows, whose commanders ordered them to attack the archers at the beginning of the battle, and ride them down under their horses' hooves; but this order was not carried out, as events showed.

Both sides had drawn up their battle lines as Sunday dawned, when a certain cardinal Périgord came to the prince, and adjured him out of respect for God who died on the Cross and for love of His mother the Virgin, and out of reverence for holy Church and in order to save the shedding of Christian blood, to suspend action for as long as was needed in order to open peace negotiations, promising future honour from his intervention if he was indeed allowed to intervene. The prince, in no way terrified by the usurper, neither feared battle nor turned away peace; but he modestly agreed to the holy father's request. So during that whole day, set aside for making peace, the French army increased by a thousand men at arms and many more common people. The following day, Monday, the cardinal returned seeking a year's truce on the part of the usurper, which the prince refused: but at the cardinal's great insistence he offered a truce to last until Christmas. So the cardinal returned to the usurper and proposed that he should give pledges for the truce offered by the prince; the marshal of Clermont advised the usurper to agree to his request, but marshal d'Audrehem, Geoffrey de Charny and Douglas the Scot objected, and the usurper strongly agreed with them. The latter claimed that in the ordinary course of events the English could not possibly win, because they were few in number, did not know the country, and were exhausted by their labours. Against them the French knights were numerous, were defending their own lands, were provided with all kinds of supplies, and had been well rested. Their courage ought to be all the greater because the king was with them, and the grace he had obtained by his coronation and anointing with holy oil would now be felt for the first time, besides the blessing of the reverend bishops of Sens and Chalons fighting under him: indeed his opponents were practically guilty of *lèse-majesté*. Realising that the usurper agreed with these arguments, Marshal de Clermont offered to the cardinal apostolic letters, by the authority of which he, Clermont, was given confession and absolution, to show that he was faithful, and so that the others would be less inclined to blame him for trying to make a truce, he asked to lead the first assault, which marshal d'Audrehem was trying to claim as his by right, supporting his claim by his slanders, which were made out of envy.

So, as the marshals argued and strove to leave each other behind, the prince learnt from the cardinal's messengers that the French leader in no way wanted peace, except by the fury of war.

*Baker goes on to describe how the prince made two speeches 'in words something like this'. The orations he gives are almost certainly his own compositions, and are best savoured in John Stow's translation (in his* Annals) *of the second speech, to the archers:*

'Your manhood (saith he) hath bin alwaies known to me, in great dangers, which sheweth that you are not degenerate from true sonnes of English men, but to be descended from the blood of them which heretofore were under my fathers dukedome and his predeccessors, kings of England, unto whom no labor was paineful, no place invincible, no ground unpassable, no hill (were it never so high) inaccessible, no tower unscaleable, no army impenetrable, no armed souldiour or whole host of men was formidable. Their lively couragiousnesse tamed the Frenchmen, the Ciprians, the Syracusians, the Calabrians, and the Palestines, and brought under the stiffe necked Scots and unruly Irishmen, yea, and the Welchmen also, which could well endure all labor. Occasion, time, and dangers maketh of fearefull men very strong and stoute, and doth many times of dull witted men make wittie: honour also, and love of the countrey, and the desire of the rich spoyle of the Frenchmen, doth stirre you up to follow your fathers steps. Wherefore followe your antientes and wholy be intentive to follow the commandement of your captaines, as well in minde as in body, that if victorie come with life, we may still continue in firme frendship together, having alwayes one will and one minde: but if envious Fortune (which God forbid) should let us at this present, to runne the race of all flesh, and that we ende both life and labour together, be you sure that your names shall not want eternall fame and heavenly joy, and we also, with these gentlemen our companions, will drinke of the same cuppe that you shall doe, unto whom it shall be an eternall glory and name to have wonne the nobilitie of France: but to be overcome (as God forbid) is not to be ascribed unto the danger of time but to the courage of the men.'

With such words, he surveyed the scene, and saw that to one side there was a nearby hill encircled by hedges and ditches outside but clear inside, for part of it was pasture and bramble-thickets, part of it planted with vines, and the rest sown fields. In these fields he believed the French army to be drawn up. Between our men and the hill was a broad deep valley and marsh, watered by a stream. The prince's battalion crossed the stream at a fairly narrow ford with their carts and leaving the valley, occupied the hill beyond the marshes and ditches, where they easily concealed their positions among the thickets, lying higher than the enemy. The field in which our vanguard and centre were stationed was separated from the level ground which the French army occupied by a long hedge and ditch, whose other end reached down to the marsh already mentioned. The earl of Warwick, in command of the vanguard, held the slope down to the marsh. In the upper part of the hedge, well away from the slope, there was a certain open space or gap, made by the carters in autumn, a stone's throw away from which our rearguard was positioned, under the command of the earl of Salisbury. The enemy, seeing the prince's banner at first displayed and then successively moving away and hidden by the line of the hill, believed that he had fled, though Douglas the Scot and Marshal de Clermont denied this. Marshal d'Audrehem, deceived by his own opinion, set out in pursuit of the prince, who he believed to have fled, and Douglas went with him, eager to confirm the glory of his new knighthood, while Clermont was eager to clear himself of any earlier imputations; these two were in command of the vanguard. As usual, the mounted lancers advanced in front; they were met by horsemen from our vanguard who were placed at the foot of the hill to meet such an attack. Marshal d'Audrehem held back his attack to see what happened in this encounter. Meanwhile, Clermont, hoping to get through the gap in the hedge and take our vanguard in the rear, met the earl of Salisbury, who, on seeing Clermont advance, guessed his intention. So the rearguard hurried to occupy the gap in the hedge to prevent the enemy from coming through it, and became the first to go into action. Then a harsh struggle between the men at arms followed, fighting with swords, lances and axes. Nor did the archers neglect their duty, but positioned in safe trenches along the ditch and beyond the hedge, they made their arrows prevail over the soldiers' armour, and shot them faster and thicker than the bolts of the crossbowmen. So our rearguard at the top of the hill near the gap engaged the enemy, and the vanguard under the earl of Warwick resisted French attackers lower down the slope and in the marsh, where the cavalry could not reach them; but they were of little use there. For the cavalry, designed to ride down the archers and protect their companions from them, stood beside the other French troops and offered the archers as a target only their forequarters, which were well protected by steel plates and leather shields, so that the arrows aimed at them either shattered, or glanced off heavenwards, falling on friend and foe alike. The earl of Oxford saw this and left the prince to lead the archers to one side, ordering them to fire at the horses' rearquarters; when this was done, the wounded chargers reared, throwing their riders, or turned back on their own men, trampling to death not a few of their masters

who had intended a quite different conclusion. Once the warhorses
were out of the way, the archers took up their previous position
and fired directly at the French flank. The horrid rage of war continued; the earls of Warwick and Salisbury competed to see which
should make the land of Poitou drink the most French blood and
each gloried in staining his own weapon with warm blood. Nor
did Thomas Ufford, earl of Suffolk, fail in his duty, full of soldierly
wisdom and renowned for his great deeds from youth to advanced
age. Passing through each line, he encouraged and urged on individuals, saw that fiery young men did not advance against orders,
and that the archers did not waste arrows; his courageous spirit
added fire to his venerable voice. Clermont, fighting bravely, met a
not unavenged death, disdaining flight or surrender. D'Audrehem
was forced to flee; William Douglas was wounded and fled, leading
a handful of his company of Scots with his brother Archibald. Almost all of them were killed in the heat of battle, and the remainder
forced either to meet an honest death or to flee, because ransoming
was excluded. But our leaders ordered that the victors should on no
account pursue the fugitives, rightly believing that even though the
beginning of the battle had gone well, the hardest work would come
when the other battalions came up. Our men refreshed themselves
and the vanguard and centre now merged.

The next French battalion advanced without delay, led by the
eldest son of the French king, namely the Dauphin of Vienne. This
battalion seemed more fierce and frightening than that which had
just been defeated; yet it could not strike fear into the hearts of our
men, eager for honour and for revenge for the wounds inflicted
earlier on them and their comrades. Both sides met boldly, roaring
out the names of St George and St Denis in the hope that they
would sway the battle in their favour. Soon the fighting was hand to
hand, each man prepared to meet his death; as swiftly as a lioness
with cubs frightens a wolf or a tiger terrifies its prey, our noble men
at arms slew or put to flight the enemy. Although this new wave of
attackers resisted our men for a long while, after much slaughter of
their men, the wiser among them became cautious and began what
the invincible French would call 'a fair retreat' rather than a flight.
Our men, however, realising that the honours of the field were still
dubious as long as the usurper and his forces might still be hidden

in some nearby valley, did not leave their places to pursue the fugitives.

But that hero worthy of his illustrious line, Sir Maurice Berkeley, son of Sir Thomas, thought otherwise. He had served throughout the prince's expedition, for both years, with his men under his own banner, and was always in the forefront of the battle. Attacking the foremost of the enemy he did deeds worthy of eternal praise against the French. He plunged into the Dauphin's battalion and laid about him with his sword, not thinking of flight so long as a Frenchman remained standing in his sight. He never looked back to see where his men were, nor looked at the standards in the air, but pursued the Dauphin's soldiers alone. Having broken his lance, sword and other weapons on them by the strength of his blows, he was over-powered by force of numbers, and taken for ransom, horribly wounded and unconscious.

Meanwhile our men placed their wounded beneath the thickets and hedges, while others took lances and daggers from the fallen to replace their own broken weapons and the archers hastened to pull their arrows out of wretches who were still half-alive. There was no-one who was not either wounded or exhausted by his labours, save for the four hundred men under the prince's banner kept in reserve to meet the usurper and his soldiers.

When the Dauphin had fled, someone who was watching the fighting came to the usurper and said: 'My lord, the English hold the field, and your eldest son has retreated.' By way of answer, the usurper swore an inviolable oath that he would not abandon the battlefield that day unless taken or killed and removed by force. So he ordered his banners to advance; followed by numerous armed men, he left the valley and presented himself to our watching army in a broad open field. A knight of great courage standing near the prince began to despair of defeating so many men, and exclaimed: 'Ah, we're beaten!' The prince, trusting in Christ and His mother the Virgin Mary, answered: 'You're a liar and a fool! How can you say we're beaten while I'm still alive?' But our men were frightened not only by the numbers of the enemy but also by their own consider-ably weakened state. Many of our men had had to withdraw from the fighting because they were wounded, the rest were very tired, and the archers had used up their arrows. So the captal de Buch, a very brave man, as soon as he saw the usurper's battalion advance, asked the prince if he could retire with sixty knights and a hundred archers; many of our men thought they were fleeing. Our army, except for the leaders, despaired of victory because of this, and commended themselves to God; regarding their lives as worthless, they only thought of dying together and to some purpose. Then the prince ordered his standard bearer, Sir Walter Woodland, to actually advance against the enemy; and with a handful of men he met the usurper's great army. The trumpets sounded and clarions, warhorns and drums replied, until the sounds echoed along the Poitevin woods, until the hills seemed to roar to the valleys and the clouds of thunder. Nor did these thunders lack thunderbolts, for the light sparkled golden on the armour, and the flying spears cascaded from polished shields, their points finding their mark like thunderbolts. Then the threatening mob of crossbowmen darkened the sky with a dense mist of bolts, and the archers replied with a hail of arrows from the English side, who were now in a state of desperate fury. Ashwood javelins flew through the air to greet the enemy at a distance, and the dense troops of the French army protecting their bodies with joined shields, turned their faces away from the missiles. So the archers emptied their quivers in vain, but, armed with swords and shields, they attacked the heavily armed enemy, anxious to buy death dearly since they expected to meet their end that day. Then the prince of Wales himself went into action, hewing at the French with his sharp sword, cutting lances, parrying thrusts, bringing the enemy's efforts to nothing, raising the fallen and teaching the enemy what the true fury of war meant.

Meanwhile the captal de Buch made a wide sweep, retreating down the slope of the hill which he and the prince had recently left and circling the battlefield, reached a point below the original position of the usurper. From there he rode up to the battlefield by the path just taken by the French, and suddenly burst out of hiding, signalling his presence to our men with the noble banner of St George. Then the prince fought to break the French line of battle before the captal attacked the French in the rear. So –

> By some heroic urge, the prince's men
> Strike in the thick of the targes, seeking a way

through the enemy's arms, safely covering their breasts with shields – and the prince divided the enemy line, laying all waste with his sword, to meet them. He plunged into the thick of the enemy –

> Savagely whirling
> His sword everywhere;
> Wounding some,
> Slaying others,
> Destroying all
> Touched by his weapon.

The unfortunate enemy were now attacked from all sides; the captal de Buch and his companions tore at them from the rear, and the archers he had taken with him wrought great havoc. The French battle line was completely broken up.

> Here prince Edward strewed in rage his bolts
> Still eager in desire to slay as many men

as he could slay among the enemy. He rushed through the confusion of the battle line, sending those he met in hand-to-hand fighting vanquished to the underworld, and hastened threateningly towards the usurper's bodyguard, still in closely order behind their solid shields. Then banners and their bearers began to fall; here men trampled on their own guts, others spat out their teeth; many were hewn to the ground, lost limbs while still standing. Dying men rolled in the blood of others, groaned under the weight of the fallen, and with proud hearts, groaned as they left their unworthy bodies. The blood of slaves and princes ran down in one stream to em-purple the nearby river and frighten the fish with this delicate nectar. Thus the boar of Cornwall raged, who –

> In shed blood only
> Found cause for rejoicing,

and reached the place where the usurper held out. Here he found a grim resistance from the bravest of men. The English fought: the French fought back, whose leader, although full of years, showed the zeal of a young knight, doing great deeds, training some, killing others, cutting or bruising faces, gutting or beheading others. He showed by everything he did that he was no unworthy descendant of the French kings. But the wheel of fortune whirled round, and the prince of Wales charged into the enemy with the wild courage of a lion; he tamed their pride, spared the fallen and accepted the surrender of the usurper.

Meanwhile the French were scattered across the Poitevin countryside, and, realising that the standard of the lilies had fallen, they fled as fast as they could to the nearby city (of Poitiers). The English, although either badly wounded or extremely weary, out of joy at having saved their lives and won the day, pursued the French up to the gates. There in a dangerous encounter they slaughtered many of the defeated French; and yet more would have perished if they had not been more eager to take prisoners for ransom than they had been in the battle.

When the trumpet call had summoned our men together again, they pitched tents in the cornfields and the whole army at once turned to the care of the wounded, rest for the weary, security for their prisoners and refreshment for the hungry. Realising that some men were missing from their midst, they sent out search parties to find them and bring them back, alive or dead, to the camp. So if anyone feared for the safety of a missing friend, he hurried to the battlefield to find him; and among the heaps of the dead they found them, hardly breathing, having freely strewn and spilt their own blood in the English king's cause, for the prince's honour and the safety of the army. Several of them nobly gave their lives for their friends, and so gained the greatest prize of charity, as truly promised by holy men, the kingdom of heaven itself.

Among those half dead and scarcely breathing was found Sir James Audley; placed on a broad shield, and carried reverently by his companions in arms, he was borne to the prince's lodgings. His whole household were thankful that he had been found, and the prince left his seat next to the king, with whom he was about to dine; he brought him back to life by his praiseworthy attention, and almost in tears kissed the cold lips, stained with blood, of his scarcely breathing friend. The prince had him stripped of his armour and laid in a soft bed, where he gradually recovered his senses, and the prince comforted him by telling him that he had captured the king, which the wounded man would hardly have believed if anyone except the prince had told him. The prince returned to the king begging him not to consider it an unworthy action of his in leaving him at dinner, because he had gone to attend a man near to death who had spared neither his blood nor his own safety in exposing himself to danger for the prince's honour. The king, learning what arms Sir James bore on his shield, said that the strength and endurance of its owner had stood out even in such a fierce battle. Little else was said at supper except that the king replied to the prince's efforts to comfort his noble captive in words similar to these: 'Although we have met with an inevitable and sad fate, at least we have come to it worthily; for although we have been conquered in battle by our noble cousin, at least we were not captured like a criminal or cowardly fugitive hiding in a corner, but, like a stout-hearted soldier ready to live and die for a just cause, we were taken on the field by the judgement of Mars, where rich men were held to ransom, cowards fled ignominiously and the bravest of all gave up their lives heroically.'

# 6. Campaign letters: the battle of Najera

*The prince's letter after the battle of Najera is a brief note sent two days after the action to Joan of Kent, then at Bordeaux, to announce the victory and to reassure her that all was well. The original letter was found in the Public Record Office in 1920. For details of the campaign, see Chandos Herald's account, which follows.*

My dearest and truest sweetheart and beloved companion, as to news, you will want to know that we were encamped in the fields near Navarrete on the second of April, and there we had news that the Bastard of Spain and all his army were encamped two leagues from us on the river at Najera. The next day, very early in the morning, we moved off towards him, and sent out our scouts to discover the Bastard's situation, who reported to us that he had taken up his position and prepared his troops in a good place and was waiting for us. So we put ourselves into battle order, and did so well by the will and grace of God that the Bastard and all his men were defeated, thanks be to our Lord, and between five and six thousand of those who fought were killed, and there were plenty of prisoners, whose names we do not know at present, but among others are Don Sancho, the Bastard's brother, the count of Denia, Bertrand du Guesclin, the marshal d'Audrehem, Don Juan Ramirez, 'Johan de Neville', 'Craundon', Lebegue de Villaines, Senor Carrillo, the Master of Santiago, the Master of Saint John and various castellans whose names we do not know, up to two thousand noble prisoners; and as for the Bastard himself, we do not know at present if he was taken, dead, or escaped. And after the said battle we lodged that evening in the Bastard's lodgings, in his own tents and we were more comfortable there than we have been for four or five days, and we stayed there all the next day. On the Monday, that is, the day when this is being written, we moved off and took the road towards Burgos; and so we shall complete our journey successfully with God's help. You will be glad to know, dearest companion, that we, our brother Lancaster and all the nobles of our army are well, thank God, except only Sir John Ferrers, who did much fighting.

# 7. Chandos Herald: Life of the Black Prince

This poem of 4000 lines survives in two manuscripts, neither of which carries a title. The author names himself in the conclusion of the work, and a reference to the Spanish campaign as happening 'not twenty years ago' places the date of composition between 1376 and 1387. Beyond this, however, we are left with conjectures. Chandos Herald was the herald of Sir John Chandos, the prince's closest companion and his friend since boyhood. From the language of the poem he has been shown to come from Hainault; in other words, he was a compatriot of queen Philippa and of Jean Froissart, and Froissart often mentions him as a source. Froissart's account of the Spanish campaign, which takes up most of the poem, is directly derived from his information. After the death of Sir John Chandos in 1370, he entered royal service, and was made king-of-arms of England by Richard II at his coronation in 1377. The poem may possibly have been written for Richard II, though if this was the case it is surprising not to find a dedication to him.

Chandos Herald's work is not a strictly historical work, but belongs to the tradition of rhyming chronicles in the common tongue which can be found from the twelfth century onwards, ranging from verse accounts of single episodes written by minstrels to full-scale romantic histories such as Wace's *Roman de Rou*, on the Normans and their ancestors. The imbalance in the content of the work makes it tempting to suggest that it may have begun as a poem on the Spanish campaign and was extended after the prince's death to cover all his exploits. There is certainly a marked contrast between the precision of the later parts and the brief or vague descriptions of the battles of Crécy and Poitiers, and the frequent use of literary conventions to describe atmosphere or feelings.

The poem has a further interest, however, as a document showing how the Black Prince was already seen as a heroic figure from some vanished golden age within a few years of his death, during the troubles of Richard's reign. During his lifetime, high hopes had been placed in him as a worthy, if not greater succcessor to his father; and when he died, men mourned the passing of those visions of future prosperity. A decade later, Chandos Herald's poem is a lament for a lost era when England was victorious and every knightly ideal seemed to be fulfilled.

# Chandos Herald

*Here begins part of the life and deeds of arms of the most noble prince of Wales and Aquitaine named Edward, son of king Edward the third, on whose soul may God have mercy.*

We learn that in days gone by those who made fine poems were regarded as authors or in some sort recorders, who set down their knowledge of good deeds, remembered such things in their heart, and were hosts to honour. But the saying goes, and indeed it is plain, that everything withers; alone among trees the tree of life does not do so, but buds and flowers in every field. But I will not linger on this subject any longer; for such things are not valued any more, and people prefer chatterers, false liars, jongleurs or jesters who will pull faces and imitate a monkey to make them laugh, to someone who can tell true stories. Such people are not welcome at court nowadays; but whatever people think of them they should not give up writing poems about good deeds, if they know how to, but should write them in a book, so that when they are dead there is an honest record. For telling of good deeds is like alms and charity: it is never lost labour, but always has its return. So I want, as my desire impels me, to make a record of the fair poems of today and yesterday.

*Now the substance of the poem begins.*

Now it is time to begin the matter in hand and to come to the point. May God let me accomplish it, because I want to set to work to record the life of the most valiant prince in all the world, the most valiant there has been since the time of Charlemagne, Julius Caesar or Arthur, as you shall hear if you listen with a good heart. It is the life of a noble prince of Aquitaine who was son of the noble king

Edward – no coward himself – and of queen Philippa, the perfect root of all honour, nobility, wisdom, valour and generosity.

*Of the noble condition of the prince.*

The noble prince of whom I speak never, from the day of his birth, thought of anything but loyalty, noble deeds, valour and goodness, and was endowed with prowess. Of such high spirit was this prince that he wished all his life to maintain justice and right, and he was brought up from childhood like this. From his own noble and open nature he learned to be generous, for his heart was always gay and noble, even from the beginning of his life and in his youth. Now it is time indeed that I started on my story, and told how noble, brave, valiant, courteous and wise he was, and how he loved holy church well, and above all the Holy Trinity; he kept the solemn feast of the Trinity from his earliest days, and kept it up all his life.

*Of the crossing of the king and the prince his son to Normandy with many noble lords* (1346).

Now I have tried to record his youth, so it is right that I should turn to what everyone esteems, namely, chivalry: he honoured it, and it reigned in him for thirty years. He used his time nobly, for I dare say that since Christ was born, there was no-one more valiant of body, as you will hear from what follows. You know how the noble king his father made war on the kingdom of France with a great army and with all his great power, saying that the crown should be his; and in keeping up this quarrel he waged a fierce war which lasted a long while. Now it happened that just then he crossed the sea to Normandy with many noble lords, barons, banneret and earls. He arrived in the Cotentin, and had many noble knights with him. The earl of Warwick, who deserves a poem to himself, the earl of Northampton, a noble person, the earls of Suffolk and Stafford, who were stout-hearted, the earl of Salisbury and the earl of Oxford too. There as well were John Beauchamp, Ralph Cobham, Sir Bartholomew de Burghersh, who did many noble deeds, and the good Guy de Brian, Richard de la Vache and Richard Talbot, who was full of prowess; Chandos and Audley were there, both expert with the sword, and good Thomas Holland, of great prowess, as well as many others whose names I do not know.

*How the English army arrived in the Cotentin, and the prince and other lords were knighted, and how the king of France heard of it.*

The English host arrived; and just as he was about to land the king knighted the prince and the earl of March, the earl of Salisbury and his brother John Montagu and others. The marshal of France Bertrand was there, who was brave and valiant, and thought he would stop them from landing, But the English troops landed by force. Such deeds of arms were done there that Roland and Oliver and Ogier le Danois, who was so courteous, might have met their match. Men of worth, bold and insolent, could be seen there. The noble and gentle prince was there too, and made a fine beginning as a knight. He made a raid across the Cotentin, burning everything and laying waste, from La Hogue, Barfleur, Carentan, Saint Lô, Bayeux and as far as Caen, where he took the bridge. There he had a great battle, and took the town by force; and the counts of Tancarville and Eu were taken prisoner. The noble prince won fame there, for he was eager to do well and was only eighteen. The marshal rode without stopping to Paris, and told the news to the king, to whom it was very unwelcome. He was so surprised that he hardly believed it, because he did not think that such men could be so daring. Then he gathered his forces; neither duke nor count remained in all France, baron, bachelor or banneret, who did not gather then.

*How the king of France sent to the king of Bohemia for help, and the king of Bohemia came, and how the English crossed the bridge at Poissy and rode through Caux.*

The king sent to the king of Bohemia, who was a good friend of his, and he brought with him his son, the king of Germany and Jean de Beaumont of Hainault who was much esteemed. He intended to defend his land from the English king; he thought little of him, and made threats against him. After this, I believe, the king and the prince raided together across Normandy, laying waste the countryside. They had many great skirmishes and took many brave men. They came to the bridge at Poissy, but the story says that the bridge was broken. However, they repaired the bridge with great beams, which very much surprised the French, and crossed it one morning. They made their way through Caux, burning, laying waste, and driving out the inhabitants, until the French were full of sorrow, and exclaimed: 'Where is Philip, our king?'

*How the king of France assembled his forces at Paris to meet the king of England and his host, and how the king of England and his forces crossed the Somme.*

Philip was at Paris, preparing his great army which was assembling there. He declared that he would think badly of himself if he did not have his revenge, because he reckoned on trapping the English between the Seine and the Somme and fighting them there. But the English amused themselves by burning everything. They made many women widows and many poor children orphans. They rode day and night until they came to the river Somme. On the other side there were many men, because the communes of Picardy were there, and Sir Godemar de Fay. The river was very wide, swollen by the tide, and the English wondered how they would cross. But the noble prince chose a hundred knights, the best of his vanguard, and sent them to see how they cross. And these praiseworthy men rode all around until they found someone who showed them a ford across the Somme. And all hundred of them went into the water at once on their war-horses – for they were valiant knights – their lances in rest, and the prince, who was following them closely, came afterwards. They had a great skirmish at the ford across the Somme, and the knights fought hard; both sides plied their bows and lances, but soon the Picards were put to flight, as well as Sir Godemar; and with God's help, all the English crossed there in due course.

*How the king of France came with three kings and his great forces to Crécy to fight the English.*

When king Philip heard this, he was sad at heart and angry, and said: 'By St Paul, I suspect treason'; but just the same he set out in haste, and passed through Abbeville. His array was very rich, for with him were three other kings, those of Majorca and Bohemia, and the king of Germany; there were dukes and counts enough. They rode without delay to a place near Crécy in Ponthieu, where they stayed. King Edward was encamped there with the prince, who commanded the vanguard that day. They had scarcely halted there when both sides were told that the other was so close that their array and order could be seen. Then the battle-cries went up and they began to set out their battalions and plan their tactics.

*The battle of Crécy: how the king of Bohemia, the duke of Lorraine, eight counts and many others were killed in the battle itself, and three kings and many others went away defeated.*

That day the battle took place, so horrible that even the boldest man would have been frightened by it. The sight of the mighty forces of the king of France was a great marvel! Full of hatred and anger, the armies met, and plied their weapons in such knightly fashion that so fierce a battle had never been seen since Christ's coming. Many banners were to be seen there, embroidered with fine gold and silk; and all the English were on foot, like men eager and ready to fight. The good prince was there, leading the vanguard, and he behaved so valiantly that it was a wonder to see. He scarcely gave anyone a chance to attack, however bold and strong he was. They fought that day until the English had the better of it: and the noble and courteous king of Bohemia was killed there, and the good duke of Lorraine, who was a most noble captain, the noble count of Flanders, the count of Alençon, brother to king Philip, and the counts of Joigny* and Harcourt. A king, a duke and seven counts, more than 60 bannerets were killed there; three kings left the field, many others fled – how many I do not know, and it is not right to count them. But I know for certain that that day the brave and noble prince had the vanguard, and we should remember it, because it was through him and his qualities that the field was won.

*How after the battle of Crécy the king of France made his way to Paris, and the king of England and his host went towards Calais.*

King Philip went to Paris, full of sorrow, regretting his rashness and the men he had lost, and the noble and worthy king of England en-camped that night on the battlefield where he had won such a great honour. He had the dead inspected, so that they could be recognised and he could be told; and they found the king of Bohemia lying dead in the fields. The king had him put into a coffin and placed on a litter covered in cloth of gold. He sent him back to the enemy, and

* An error: he was captured before the battle.

then moved on from that place, riding towards Calais. This noble raid of which I am speaking was made in 1346, and the king fought this battle, where he acquired such fame, on the eve of St Bartholomew.*

*How the king of England and his great army besieged Calais for eighteen months and the king of France did not dare raise the siege, so that the town surrendered to the king of England.*

Then they came to Calais, where many fine deeds were done. There the noble king and all his army besieged the town for eighteen months† without a break. They stayed there so long that there was famine in the town, and king Philip came in haste to raise the siege. But the army was so entrenched, and the town so closely besieged, that king Philip did not dare to raise the siege, and the king of England held that land. Many skirmishes and assaults were made there both on top of the walls and at the foot, until the town surrendered, begging the king to show them mercy. Thus Calais was conquered by force of arms by the troops of the noble king and his bold son the prince.

*How the king of England and his army returned to England; how the town of Calais would have been surrendered to the French by treason; and how the king of England and his men resisted this plot in such a way that he would have been captured if he had not been rescued by his son the prince.* (1349–50)

After this, the king and the prince and all their bold knights hardly wanted to return to England. They stayed in their own country because of a truce they had made, until it happened that by a treacherous and wicked agreement Calais was to be sold to the lord of Beaujeu and Geoffrey de Charny, by a Lombard called Aimeric de Pavia; and the greater part of the barons of Picardy and France were there. But the king was also there, and the noble prince his son who fought so valiantly that night that he rescued his father the king. The French and the men of Picardy were put to flight that night, and many English welcomed their own men when they returned, for all the best knights of England were there, who did valiant deeds in order to win praise and renown. The most noble barons of France

* i.e. 23 August. In fact, the battle was fought on 26 August.
† In fact eleven months (September 1346–August 1347).

were captured there, and completely outwitted; but the king of England never had so much to do at any time as he did then, for many people have recorded that the king would have been captured if it had not been for the prince his son, whose noble strength and prowess rescued the king his father, a deed which should never be forgotten.

*How the king of England and his troops returned after Calais had been rescued, and after this there was a sea-battle in which the Spaniards were killed and defeated.* (1350)

They returned to England, with great rejoicing; their friends were joyful, and all the ladies as well. The queen, who loved her lord with all her heart, welcomed them. Then the king said to his wife, 'Lady, make your son welcome, for without him I would have been captured; but I was rescued by him.' 'He is welcome, and you as well,' she said. 'Now I can truly say that he was born in a good hour.' Knights and barons were honourably received, and there was dancing, feasting and revelling; the time passed happily, and there was love and nobleness, gaiety and prowess to be found there. So things went on for a long while, until it happened that the Spanish fleet gathered at Sluys, boasting that they would go wherever they wanted in spite of the king and his men; so the king gathered all his great barons and gathered a splendid army at sea. The prince his son and many worthy knights were there, all the earls and barons and well-known knights. The battle was fierce and hard; but God gave the prince good fortune, because he and his army valiantly killed and defeated the Spaniards. Sir John, his brother, later duke of Lancaster, was there, a valiant knight. The noble barons too behaved valiantly; many ships were conquered, taken or sunk, and many men killed, as my record says. And this battle took place outside Winchelsea.

*How after the sea-battle the queen of England gave birth to a son called Thomas; and afterwards the captal de Buch came to England to ask for the prince as their leader in Gascony, and at this the parliament ordered that the prince was to go to Gascony with several counts and other lords.*

After this noble but very horrible battle, they returned to land, with the great booty which they had won, and with which they were all delighted. A little while after this the queen of England had her last son, who was called Thomas. A great and joyful feast was held, and a great tournament proclaimed throughout the country. About then the captal de Buch came from Gascony, a valiant and noble man, very bold and brave, and popular with everyone. He was given a noble welcome, and the prince was very glad of his arrival. One day he said to the king his father, and the queen, his mother: 'Sire, you know how many noble knights in Gascony are your friends, and how they fight hard on your behalf, but have no captain of your blood. If your advisers thought fit to send one of your sons, they would be all the bolder.' So the king summoned parliament, who agreed to send the prince to Gascony, and commanded that there should go with him the noble earl of Warwick, the earl of Salisbury, who was also very valiant, Ufford, earl of Suffolk, the earl of Oxford and the earl of Stafford, Bartholomew de Burghersh, John Montagu, the lord Despenser, Basset, Sir Walter Manny, and also the good Reginald de Cobham who had been at many an assault; Chandos and Audley were there, appointed to advise the prince.

*The arrangements for the prince's voyage from Plymouth to Gascony, and how he took leave of the king his father and the queen his mother.*

When everything was planned and arranged, all the ships were ordered to gather at Plymouth, as were the men at arms and archers with provisions for them. The array was a rich one. Two months later the prince took leave of the king and queen and all his brothers and sisters; there was sorrow in their hearts when it came to his departure, and ladies and girls were to be seen weeping for their husbands and lovers.

*How the prince came to Plymouth with all his army, and stayed there until he was ready to cross; how he arrived at Bordeaux and the lords and barons of Gascony received him joyfully and with honour; how afterwards the prince took the field with six thousand men and took and laid waste several castles and villages in Gascony.* (1355)

Then the prince took his leave, with a cheerful heart; he made his way to Plymouth, riding day and night until he arrived, and stayed there until all his great army was ready. And very soon afterwards his ships were loaded with provisions and jewels, hauberks, helmets, lances, shields, bows, arrows and more besides; his horses were put aboard, and he set sail with all his noble knights. There the flower of chivalry and noble knighthood was to be seen, all eager to do great deeds. Then they set sail, and sailed across the sea to Bordeaux, where the noble barons of those parts rejoiced at their arrival. Greater and lesser lords came to the prince, who made them welcome. The prince d'Albret hastened to him, the lord of Montferrand, noble and bold-hearted, the lords of Mussidan, Rauzan, Curton and Amanieu de Fossard, the great lord of Pommiers and many noble knights, among them the lord of Lesparre. In short, all the barons of Gascony came, and the famous prince knew how to entertain them. He spent a little time at Bordeaux, until he had arrayed his army and rested his horses. He was soon ready to put an army of six thousand men into the field. He rode towards Toulouse; there were no towns which he did not lay waste. He took Carcassonne, Béziers and Narbonne, and laid waste and harried all the countryside as well as many towns and castles, which did not please his enemies in Gascony. He was in the field for four and a half months or more, and did great damage.

*How the prince returned to Bordeaux and stayed there with great rejoicings until the winter was over; meanwhile he quartered his men in all his neighbouring castles.*

Then the prince returned to Bordeaux and stayed there until the winter was past. He and his noble knights lived in great happiness and joy. There were gay, noble, courteous, good and generous men there: and he put his men in winter quarters in the castles nearby. Warwick was at La Réole, Salisbury at Ste Foy, Suffolk at St Emilion, and his men were lodged at Libourne and all around. When they were quartered like this, Chandos and Audley, always eager for fame, with the noble and loyal captal went on a long campaign, making many fine skirmishes and often fighting to find somewhere to lodge. They made a raid as far as Cahors and Agen, and took Porte Ste Marie. Then they came back up the river and went to take Périgord, a famous city. There they lodged for a great part of the winter; and it was a noble visit, for they made many attacks and assaults on the castle. There was only a little meadow separating it from the town, and the count de l'Isle and the count of Périgord were its defenders.

*How the prince reassembled his forces and rode into Saintonge and other parts of Gascony, taking certain fortresses and lords before the battle of Poitiers; and how the news came to the king of France.* (1356)

Thus the prince stayed in Gascony for more than eight months. When it came to the summer, he gathered his forces and made another raid into Saintonge, Périgord and Quercy, as far as Romorantin. There he took the keep by storm, and captured lord Boucicaut, the great lord de Craon and a great number of others, more than two hundred in all, all of them men at arms of great worth, and this a fortnight before the battle of Poitiers. Then he rode through Berry and Gascony as far as Tours in Touraine. News of this came to king John, who was very sad to hear it, and swore to take his vengeance.

*How the king of France gathered a great army at Chartres to meet the prince and his army, and the prince marched to Poitiers, where he took two counts and killed many other men.*

Then he gathered all the forces of the kingdom of France; there was neither duke nor count nor baron of note whom he did not summon, and they all assembled at Chartres. He brought together a noble army; according to the list he had more than ten thousand. They left Chartres and rode in haste to Tours. The prince heard of this, and the news was welcome to him. He made his way to Poitiers, carrying much booty with him, for they had done much damage in France by their raid. On the Saturday the prince captured the count of Joigny and the count of Auxerre; although the French fought valiantly at their encampment, they were all either killed or taken, as the book says. The English army were very pleased by this. King John rode on until he had overtaken the prince, and, so I have heard, they encamped so close to each other that they watered their horses in the same river.

*How the cardinal of Périgord came to the king of France with many clergy to make peace between him and the prince, and having heard the king of France's opinion the cardinal rode to the prince for the same reason.*

But the cardinal of Périgord arrived, and with him many clergy and lawyers. He said gently to the king of France, in all humility: 'Sire, for the love of God, listen to timely advice. Allow me to ride to the prince and speak to him to see if you can come to an agreement. Otherwise there will be a great and horrible battle, and much loss and damage will be done. It is a great pity that so many fine men should be sent to their deaths; but they will be unless you can be reconciled. And he who is in the wrong will have to answer for all this to God at the Day of Judgement.' King John replied: 'Cardinal, you are very wise, and we wish you to go to the prince; but we shall never make peace unless the castles and lands that he has wrongfully ravaged and laid waste since he left England are returned to us, and unless he abandons the quarrel for which he has started the war again.' 'Sire,' said the cardinal, 'I shall do all I can to secure your rights and satisfy you.' And he left him.

*How the cardinal rode from the king of France to the prince's army to negotiate the aforementioned agreement.*

He rode to the prince's army, and as soon as he arrived, greeted the prince gently, and wept for pity: 'Sire,' he said, 'take pity on all those noble men who might lose their lives here today in this great conflict. Are you sure that you are not in the wrong? If you would make an agreement, God and the Holy Trinity would reward you for it.'

*The prince's answer to the cardinal about the proposed agreement.*

The prince said: 'Indeed, good father in God, we know that what you say is true, and is in the Scriptures. But we maintain that our quarrel is just and true. You know that it is no idle story that my father, king Edward, was the nearest heir, who should have held France, and to whom everyone should have done allegiance, at the time when Philip of Valois was crowned king. But despite this, I do not want to say that so many brave men died here because I was proud. Nor do I ever mean to hinder peace, and will do all I can to further it. But I cannot do anything final without the king, my father, though I can give my men time to talk longer about a peace. If they do not want peace, I am ready to await God's verdict, for our quarrel is so just that I am not frightened of fighting. But if the damage and losses and deaths can be avoided, I will agree, if my father also agrees.'

*How the cardinal went weeping from the prince and returned to the king of France and told him of his negotiations and how the king of France gave bishops and lords the task of negotiating to avoid a battle.*

The cardinal left him, weeping, and rode at once to king John, and told him of his negotiations. The king, to delay matters and postpone the battle, brought together the barons of both sides, and spoke to them at length. The count of Tancarville, and according to the list, the archbishop of Sens and Jean de Talaru, Charny, Boucicaut and Clermont were deputed on the French side.

*How the prince gave English lords the task of negotiating a treaty with the French.*

On the other side, the earl of Warwick, the grey-haired earl of Suffolk, Sir Bartholomew de Burghersh, the prince's closest adviser, and Audley and Chandos, were chosen. All of them met and spoke their minds; what they said I do not know, but they could not agree, or so I have heard. Then Geoffrey de Charny said: 'Lords, as you cannot agree terms, I offer a combat of a hundred against a hundred, each side to choose their own; and whoever are the losers will leave the field and abandon the conflict. This would be the best solution, and God would favour it, because it would avoid the deaths of many noble men.'

*The final answer of the English to the French negotiators. How the lords appointed to negotiate returned to their own sides without reaching agreement, and how the cardinal rode away weeping to Poitiers.*

And then the earl of Warwick replied: 'My lord, what do you want to gain by this? You know that you are four times as many as us in numbers of men at arms, well equipped, and that it is your land we are raiding. Look at this field and our positions, and let each do the best he can: I offer no other arrangement. Let God help those who are most in the right!' Then they separated, without another word, and returned to their own armies. Each side said, 'This cardinal has betrayed us'; but it was not true, for he went off weeping and rode to Poitiers, as he needed to, because neither side thanked or liked him for his efforts. Then each side prepared immediately for battle.

*How the king of France assigned the Marshal de Clermont, several other lords, three thousand men at arms, two thousand followers and two thousand crossbowmen to be the vanguard.*

The king of France first marshalled his men and said: 'Lords, I swear you are delaying me so much that the prince is going to escape me. This cardinal has betrayed me by making me wait so long.' Then he began by summoning marshal of Clermont and the much-praised marshal d'Audenham, who was a good knight, and the duke d'Athènes, a noble captain. 'Lords,' the king said, 'draw up your men, because you are to be the vanguard, as is your right. You will have with you three thousand men and two thousand followers with swords and javelins and two thousand crossbowmen as well to help you. If you find the English, give battle and do not hesitate to put them all to death.'

*How the king of France put the duke of Normandy, his son, the duke of Bourbon and several other lords with four thousand men at arms in the second battalion of his army.*

Then he summoned his son, the duke of Normandy, and said to him: 'Son, you are to be king of France after me, so you must have the second battalion, with the noble duke of Bourbon as your companion, as well as the lord of St Venant, who is valiant and stout-hearted and the noble knight Tristan de Maguelais who will carry your silken banner. Do not hesitate to put the English to death, whether they are great men or not, because I do not want a single one to go back across the sea to harm me or make war on me again.' 'I will deal with them as you tell me,' said the Dauphin, 'and we will make sure we earn your favour.' Then the banners and pennants were unfurled in the wind, purple and gold and ermine; trumpets, drums, horns and bugles rang out through the camp; the Dauphin's great battalion made the earth resound. There were many fine knights there, and as the list says, there were four thousand men in all. The battalion took up its place to one side, taking up a great deal of space, all arranged as the king had ordered.

*How the king of France assigned the duke of Orléans with three thousand men to be the rearguard of his army.*

Then he summoned his brother the duke of Orléans and said:

'Brother, you are to lead the rearguard with three thousand valiant men at arms; and make sure, in God's name, that you have no mercy on the English, but put them all to death, because they have done us much wrong, and burnt and destroyed our lands since they left England. If you take the prince, bring him straight to me.' 'My lord,' said the duke, 'I will happily do all this and more.'

*How the king of France himself with three of his sons and many counts and other lords, twenty-three banners in all, and four hundred knights mounted on armed horses formed the fourth battalion.*

King John arrayed his troops so that he was in the fourth battalion, with three of his sons, all worthy knights: the duke of Anjou, the duke of Barry, and Philip the bold, who was still very young. Jacques de Bourbon was there, the counts of Eu and Longueville, sons of Robert d'Artois; the count of Sancerre was there with the count of Dammartin. It was a splendid array, for there were twenty-three banners and four hundred knights on armed horses, all picked men, led by Guichard d'Angle, the lord d'Aubigny and Eustace de Ribemont, whom the king trusted especially. And he begged them to strike hard and do all they could to break the enemy battalion, and to support anyone who was doing great deeds. All promised to do as he said. It was marvellous to see so many nobles; indeed, so many nobles and such an array as that of the French had never been seen before.

*How the prince put his men in battle order, giving the earl of Warwick the vanguard and the earl of Salisbury the rearguard; and how he commanded Sir Eustace d'Abrichecourt and the lord of Curton to seek out the French army. They advanced so far that they were captured, and the French rejoiced greatly.*

The English army was encamped on the other side, and the prince also put his men in battle order. He would have been happy to avoid a battle, but he saw that he had got to fight. So he summoned the earl of Warwick, and told him plainly: 'My lord, we must fight today, so please take command of the vanguard. The lord of Pommiers, a noble knight, will be your companion, and you will have his brothers with you, all of them brave and bold. You are to cross the ford and guard our waggons. I will ride after you with all my knights, and if anything happens to you we will come to your aid; the earl of Salisbury will follow as well, leading our rearguard; and everyone is to be ready to dismount at once if the enemy attack.' And they all said they would do so; and so the night passed, without much comfort, because everyone was lying in wait and there were many skirmishes. When it was full daylight, the prince summoned Sir Eustace d'Abrichecourt and the lion-hearted lord of Curton, and ordered them to go out to spy out the French positions. Both rode off on their fine war-horses, but, as the book says, they went so far out of their lines that they were captured. This made the prince sad, and the French army were delighted, saying aloud: 'All the others will meet the same fate.'

*How the shouting began, and the prince moved off and rode away, not expecting to fight that day; and the French shouted to the king that the English were fleeing. But it was not true, as the French quickly discovered.*

Then the shouting began, and a great noise arose, and the prince moved off; he rode away, because he did not wish to fight that day but to avoid a battle. On the other side, the French shouted to the king that the English were fleeing and they would soon lose them. Then the French rode off without waiting any longer. Marshal d'Audrehem said: 'I don't think much of your efforts. We shall soon lose the English if we don't attack.' Marshal de Clermont answered: 'Brother, you are in too much of a hurry; do not be so hasty because we shall get there in good time. The English are not fleeing, but coming steadily towards us.' D'Audrehem said: 'Your delay will make us lose them very soon.' Then Clermont replied: 'By St Denis, marshal, you are very bold,' and added angrily: 'But you will never be bold enough to get your lance in front of my horse's backside.' So, full of bad temper, they set out towards the English.

*How the clamour began and the two armies approached each other, and the earl of Salisbury was the first to join battle, because the marshals came on him and attacked him fiercely.*

Then the clamour and shouting began, and the two armies approached each other. On both sides swords were drawn, and lances couched; no-one did not join in. The earl of Salisbury, so I am told, led the prince's rearguard; but that day he was the first to join battle, because the marshals, full of anger and bad temper, attacked him on foot and on horseback. When the earl saw their troops, he turned his battalion towards them, and cried: 'Advance, my lords, in God's name, since St George wills that although we were the last, we should be the first to fight; and let us do deeds that will win us honour.' So the barons hurled themselves into the battle; if you had no part in the battle, it would have been a fine thing to watch, but it was a sad and harsh sight as well. Many men were killed there; archers fired volleys thicker than rain on the two sides facing the armed horses. Then a noble knight called Guichard d'Angle came up; he did not keep in a corner, but charged into the mêlée, using sword and spear. And the marshal of Clermont, Eustace de Ribemont and the lord of Antigny all did great deeds.

*How the earl of Salisbury and the rearguard defeated the marshals and the armed cavalry before the vanguard could wheel round; and after this they all reassembled together and approached the Dauphin's battalion, at a gap in a little hedge; and the Dauphin was defeated, with the Normandy battalion, and the French fled, and many of them were killed and taken; and then the French king and his great forces approached the prince and his host.*

The book and the story tell how the earl of Salisbury and his companions, who fought more fiercely than lions, defeated the marshals and the armed cavalry before the vanguard could wheel round and come back over the river which they had just crossed. But they all assembled together and came on in a noble band up the hill until their ranks were facing the Dauphin's battalion, which was going through a gap in a little hedge. They came on steadily and did such deeds of arms that it was wonderful to watch. They captured the gap in the hedge by their attack, which dismayed the French, who began to turn their backs and mount their horses. There were shouts everywhere of 'Guyenne! St George!' The Normandy battalion was defeated while it was still morning and the Dauphin left the field. Many were killed and taken there; and the prince fought valiantly, urging on his men, saying 'Lords, for God's sake attack; look, here I am!' Then the king of France approached with great forces, because he had all the men with him who were most eager for glory.

*How the prince saw the king of France and his great forces approach and many of the English had left the prince to pursue the fleeing French because they thought that they had done everything; and the prince said his prayers to Almighty God and said: 'Banners, advance!' and the struggle began. Audley was the first to encounter the enemy and the English lords and Gascon barons fought the French with all their strength, and the prince had the victory by the grace of God and the French king and Philip his son and several other earls and other lords of France were taken by the English and the duke of Bourbon and many other lords, knights and squires of France; three thousand in all, were killed in this great battle.*

When the prince saw them coming, he was a little disheartened, and looking round, he saw that some of his men had gone off in pursuit of the French, because they thought that their work was done for the moment; but now the fighting was getting heavier, because of the arrival of the French king with so many troops that it was astonishing to see them. When the prince saw this he looked up to heaven and cried to Christ for mercy, saying; 'Almighty Father, as I believe that You are king of all kings and willingly endured death on the Cross to rescue us from Hell, God the Father, who is truly man, by Your most holy name protect me and my men from evil, for You know that our cause is just.' Then the prince, as soon as he had finished his prayer, said: 'Banners, advance! Let each think of his honour!' Two knights full of valour were on each side of him; these were Chandos and Audley. Audley humbly and gently made a request to the prince: 'My lord, I have vowed to God that wherever I saw the banner of the king of France among his troops, I would be the first to break a lance with them. Please give leave to go, for it is high time to attack them.' The prince said, 'James, do as you wish.' Then James left the prince at once, and set out a lance's length in front of the others, and hurled himself on the enemy like a coura-geous and bold man; but he hardly lasted a moment before he was brought to the ground. As the two sides met, you could see great lances couched and thrust on each side; all played their part; Chandos was to be seen dealing blows, and he gained great praise that day: Warwick and Despenser, worthy Montagu, Mohun and Basset, Sir Ralph de Cobham who did great damage to the French, the good Bartholomew de Burghersh, bold in his deeds; elsewhere

Salisbury and Oxford fought strongly, and also the noble barons of Gascony, the captal and the lord of Pommiers, d'Albret, Lesparre and Langoiran, Fossard and Couchon and Rauzan, Mussidan and the lord of Caupenne, Monferrand, who tries above all others to do well. These squires of noble degree could be seen giving such great blows that it was amazing to watch. The battle was very fierce, and many men were killed. The struggle lasted a long while, and the boldest man was dismayed by it; but the noble prince shouted many times: 'Lords, advance, in God's name, let us win this battle if we value our lives and honour.' The valiant prince did such deeds in his wisdom that the victory was his, and the enemy fled, and many left the field, at which king John cried out; he fought bravely and many good knights with him who wanted to help him. But strength was of little value, for the prince attacked him so fiercely that he was captured, and Philip his son as well, Jacques de Bourbon and a great number of others: the count of Eu and Charles the courteous count of Artois, the count of Dammartin, the count of Joigny, the count of Tancarville and the count of Sarrebruck, the good count Ventadour of Sancerre; all these were captured that day and many noble knights banneret whose names I do not know. From what I am told there were sixty counts and bannerets captured there and more than a thousand others whom I cannot list. And I have heard that the following were killed there: the duke of Bourbon, the duke of Athènes, the marshal of Clermont, Matas, Landas and Ribemont and the lord Renaud de Pons, and others whose names I could not tell you; but I have heard, and find in my sources, that there were more than three thousand dead. God receive their souls, for the bodies lay still on the field. The English were full of joy, shouting everywhere 'Guyenne! St George!' There were few French to be seen! Archers, knights and squires could be seen running everywhere to take prisoners. Thus were the French taken and slain that day, as my book says.

*The month and day of this great battle.*

The occasion I have spoken of was on the nineteenth of September, 1356; it was then that this great and terrible battle took place, which I have briefly spoken of.

*How king John of France was brought to the prince, and the prince gave him assistance and disarmed him, and how they talked together, and how they spent the night on the ground among the dead, and the next morning the prince set off and made his way to Bordeaux; and all the clergy of Bordeaux came out in procession to meet them; and they passed the winter in great joy at Bordeaux; and the prince sent word to the king and queen of his deeds and asked for ships to be sent to take king John to England.*

But I want to tell you about the prince, who was bold and brave, and wise in his deeds and words; king John was brought to him, and the prince welcomed him and gave thanks to Almighty God, and to do more honour to the king, wanted to help him to disarm. But the king said to him: 'Cousin, in God's name, do not trouble yourself, for I do not deserve it; and you have won more honour today than any prince before you.' The prince replied: 'My lord, God has done this and not us; and we must thank Him and pray that He will grant us His glory and pardon this victory.' So they talked, while the English celebrated. The prince spent the night on the ground, among the dead, in a little tent, with his men around him; he slept little that night. In the morning he moved off and made his way to Bordeaux, taking his prisoners with him; and all the noble knights rode on until they reached the city. They were nobly welcomed at Bordeaux by all the people; all the clergy of Bordeaux came to meet them in procession, bearing crosses and chanting prayers, and all the ladies and girls both old and young, and all the maids: there was a marvellous celebration at Bordeaux. The prince stayed there all winter, and then sent his messenger to the king and queen with news of his deeds and ordered ships to be sent to take the king of France to England.

*How the king and queen were delighted with the news sent them by the prince, and gave thanks to God; and they sent ships to Bordeaux, and the prince brought king John and the other prisoners to England and sent word to his father, who came to meet them and rode with them to London, where great feasts, celebrations and jousts were held, and they remained there happily for four years or more.*

When the king heard the news he was delighted by it and praised God, clasping his hands and saying: 'Sovereign Father, praise to You for all this good news!' and the noble queen too praised God and the Virgin because they had given her such a noble son. They dismissed the messenger, and sent to the prince ships and barges in good numbers. The ships came to Bordeaux, which pleased the prince; he did not want to wait any longer. He had all his equipment loaded on board, and all the barons and knights went to sea, and made the king and all the prisoners go on board as well. They sailed until they came to England, and as soon as they landed sent word to the king, who thought the news excellent, and ordered all his barons to form a guard of honour, and he himself went with more than twenty earls. They escorted the prince to London, where he was given a great welcome. He was greeted by the ladies, and never were there such celebrations as then. The king and queen and the king's mother were there, many ladies and many lovely, gay and loving girls. They danced, hunted, hawked, jousted and feasted, just as in King Arthur's reign, for more than four years.

*How the king of England made another journey to France with his barons and the noble prince and duke Henry and more than ten thousand others and rode through Artois and several counties of France to Paris and encamped in the fields there, but never fought a battle; and so they changed direction to Chartres where peace was agreed and sworn and king John was freed and all Guyenne was surrendered and delivered into the hands of the king of England and his son the prince. (1359)*

Then the king made another expedition to France with his barons, and the noble prince, and Henry duke of Lancaster and more than ten thousand whom I will not list; but, so the book says, he rode through Artois, Picardy, Vermandois, Champaigne, Burgundy and Brie and came to Paris. Both the king and the prince encamped there, ready for battle, but no battle took place. So they changed direction, to Chartres. There peace was agreed and later sworn; and the prince had a great deal to do with it, because it was he who got the two kings to agree. And king John was released from prison, and all Guyenne and its dependencies were awarded to the king and his son the prince. This peace of which I tell you was made in the year 1360, at the time of year when the nightingale sings, the merry month of May when birds rejoice.

*How the king of England, the prince and their troops returned to England and how the two kings later met at Calais with the prince and all the barons and*

*knights of both kingdoms, and how both sides swore to keep peace and never to
renew the war; and all returned to their own country in haste.*

They returned to England, taking their great army with them.
They were made welcome and a great feast was held. After All
Saints' Day the two kings met at Calais, the prince and all the
barons and famous knights of England, and all those of the kingdom
of France as well. They swore of their own free will on the Bible
and on the Holy Sacrament that they would keep the peace, without
treachery, and would not renew the war. So the two kings were in
agreement in making peace. The king of France went away without
staying any longer; and the king of England and the prince returned
in good spirits, taking the hostages with them.

*How the prince married a lady of great worth, who went with him later to
Gascony, where he took possession of the land and reigned there for seven
years, keeping house in high style and holding great jousts and revels; how he
had two sons; and how all the barons and lords of Gascony came to him and
did homage and loved him greatly.* (1361–70)

The prince, very soon after this, married a lady of great worth, with
whom he had fallen in love, who was beautiful, pleasing and wise.
He did not wait long after his marriage before going to Gascony to
take possession of his lands. The prince took his wife with him,
whom he loved greatly. By her he had two sons. He ruled in Gascony
for seven years, in joy, peace and happiness; for all the barons of the
lands around came to do homage; they regarded him as a wise, true
and good lord; and since Christ was born no-one ever lived in such
state and honour. Every day there were more than eighty knights
at his table and four times as many squires. They jousted and held
revels at Angoulême and Bordeaux; all the nobles were there, joyful
and happy, generous and honourable; and all his subjects and his
men loved him well because he did so much good for them. He was
much valued and esteemed by those close to him, for he was both
generous and noble, level-headed, just, reasonable and restrained:
you could honestly say that no prince like him was to be found anywhere in the world. His neighbours and enemies were very fearful
of him, because he was so valiant that his rule was powerful everywhere. Now I will tell you of a noble expedition to Spain, for
which he deserved praise, one of the most noble enterprises ever

undertaken by Christians. He restored to the throne by force of arms a king disinherited by his younger bastard brother.

*How the duke of Brittany won his lands by a battle there with the help of the English forces, and Charles de Blois and other noble lords were killed, and Bertrand du Guesclin and other brave knights taken prisoner.*

There was a battle in Brittany, where the duke and his company conquered those lands with the help of English troops, and where Charles de Blois and other noble barons of France and Picardy were killed. Bertrand du Guesclin was captured there, along with many other noble lords, whose names I will omit for the sake of brevity, and return to my story.

*How after the battle in Brittany Bertrand du Guesclin led the Great Company out of France with many other knights and squires to make an expedition to Spain, because of the lengthy war between Spain and Aragon, in which the Pope wished them to make peace between the two kings.* (1366)

You know that Sir Bertrand led all the Great Company and many other raiders out of France, by his prowess and power, as the Pope wished; and he also took with him, barons, knights, counts and squires. At this time there had long been a strange and cruel war between Spain and Aragon: it had lasted thirteen years or more. For this reason Bertrand du Guesclin, Jean de Bourbon, comte de la Marche, marshal d'Audrehem, Eustace d'Abrichecourt, Hugh Calveley, Matthew Gournay and many other true knights were chosen to go to that country to make peace between the kings, and to open the passes and mountain roads to Granada, so that they could go and conquer it. This was the arrangement, and Sir Bertrand and his men were well paid for it.

*How Bertrand du Guesclin and his company crossed the frontier of Aragon and sent word to king Pedro of Castile that they wished to pass through the country to go on crusade against God's enemies, and how the king was angry at their request and prepared to defend his land; but nonetheless they entered Spain, and Pedro was very angry, swearing that he would take vengenace. But soon afterwards king Pedro was dethroned by great treachery and fled into exile, and the Castilians crowned the bastard Enrique king of Spain.*

When they had started out, he and all his company crossed the frontier of Aragon, and soon afterwards sent word to the king of

Castile that he was to make and swear peace with Aragon, and that he was to allow them passage to go on crusade against God's enemies. But he was proud and scornful and feared little for them or anyone else, and he grew very angry at this, swearing that he would not obey such people. So he gathered an army and prepared himself to defend his country, ordering both gentlemen, freemen and villeins to come, thinking that he would certanly meet the crusaders and defend his lands. English, French, Britons, Normans, Picards, and Gascons all entered Spain, as did the Great Company; Sir Hugh Calveley and Gournay, his companion, and many other bold knights entered the kingdom and conquered all the lands which Pedro had conquered before. King Pedro of Spain was very angry at this and swore to have his revenge; but all his troops were little use to him, because within a month he was forced to flee from Spain and abandon his throne through the great treachery of his men; for all those who should have loved him betrayed him. Anyone who is not loved by his people should not be called lord: we can see this by the example of this proud king, who feared no-one and thought that none could hurt him because of his great army; but in no time at all even his friends, relations and brothers had abandoned him. They crowned his bastard brother, giving him all the land; and in Castile both great and small recognised him as lord.

*How king Pedro went to Seville, put his treasure on board ship and sailed to Corunna; and how the Bastard rode through Castile, taking possession of cities and accepting homage from its lords, all of whom agreed that he should be king except a loyal and brave knight called Fernandez de Castro.*

King Pedro did not dare wait any longer, but went at once to Seville, where his treasure was kept and had ships and galleys brought, into which the treasure was laden. He sailed day and night until he reached the port of Corunna in Galicia. The Bastard was not stupid; he rode through Castile, and no city remained outside his possessions, and no count or baron failed to do him homage, except one only, called Fernandez de Castro, a valiant and gentle man, who swore that he would never abandon the rightful king, and whatever those in power did, he could not agree to a bastard holding the kingdom. But all the others of that country agreed that Henry should be king of Castile, Toledo and Seville, Cordoba and Leon. So

Castile was conquered with the agreement of all its barons, by the forces of Bertrand du Guesclin. Now listen to what happened in the end, not twenty years ago.

*How king Pedro, at Corunna, despondent because of his misfortunes, remembered his alliance with the king of England, and relied on him and his power to help him and relieve his bitter sorrows.* (1367)

Now I have a fine story to tell, for pity, love and justice are all part of it, as you will hear. I have told you how matters stood: king Pedro was very despondent at Corunna, and bitter over his betrayal by those who should have been loyal to him. He was full of sadness, and did not know where to turn for help, despite his wealth and his gold. One day the king remembered that he had alliances and friendship of long standing with the king of England, who was a most noble king, for God had given him such virtues that no one since king Arthur's day had been so powerful, and if Edward would help him because of this alliance, and out of love and family ties, and for God's and knighthood's sake, he might yet be restored.

*How king Pedro summoned his council and Fernandez de Castro advised him to seek help from the prince.*

So he summoned his council, and laid the matter before them, and all said that he was right. Then a noble lord spoke, who was full of wisdom, Fernandez de Castro, and said: 'Sire, listen to me, by the faith I owe you, send first of all to the prince of Aquitaine, Edward's son; he is a worthy man, bold, and with such a force of men at arms that no living man can do him wrong unless God wills it; and if you find him agreeable, Spain will be in your hands before the end of the year.' All this was agreed.

*How king Pedro wrote letters to the prince, asking for his help and for ships to be sent to fetch him so that he could talk to him, and sent the letters by his messengers.*

King Pedro of Castile wrote and sealed a letter at once, begging the prince, for God's sake, and out of love, pity, alliance, friendship, ties of blood and justice, that he, the noble, powerful, valiant and honourable prince, would be pleased to assist a righteous cause and him who patiently begged this of him; and that ships would be sent to fetch him so that he could talk to him. The messengers left at once.

*How the messengers of king Pedro found the prince at Bordeaux and gave him the letters, at which the prince was very surprised, and summoned his knights and best councillors, to whom he showed the letters. They advised him on the matter, and it was ordered that men-at-arms should be sent to help king Pedro.*

The prince was at Bordeaux, and was very surprised when he had read the letter. As soon as he had seen it, he summoned his knights and all his best councillors and showed them the letters, just as they had been written, and said: 'Lords, by my faith, I am surprised at what I see here. He who trusts in his power is a fool: you have seen how France, once the most powerful land in Christendom, has been conquered by us with God and right on our side; and I have been told that the leopards and their company could reach out further, into Spain, and if it was in our days, we should be regarded as all the braver for it. Good advice on this, lords, is what we need; tell me what you think.' Chandos and Thomas Felton, his companions and closest councillors, replied that this could only be accomplished if they had an alliance with the king of Navarre, who controlled the passes into Spain. So the council agreed to send messengers to the king of Navarre and to the count of Armagnac and all the barons of Aquitaine; and after that all the prince's great council gathered. Each of them said what he thought would be best done in such a case; and in the end the council agreed to order vessels to be made ready at Bayonne, and men at arms and archers as well, to go to help king Pedro in Spain. Thomas Felton, the Seneschal of Aquitaine, was to be their captain.

*How king Pedro arrived at Bayonne, bringing with him his sons and daughters and what was left of his treasure, and how the prince went to meet him; and after this the prince and the king of Navarre agreed to help king Pedro.*

But while they were preparing and loading the ships, king Pedro himself arrived in Bayonne, with his sons and daughters, and what was left of his treasure, in jewels, pearls, gold and silver. When the prince heard this, he thought it good news. He went to meet him at Bayonne, and gave him a noble welcome; they held many great feasts there. They all, and the king of Navarre as well, agreed to help king Pedro to win back Spain; since he had so humbly asked them he deserved to be helped: on this they were unanimous, and the prince did not delay any longer.

*How the prince returned to Bordeaux and prepared his army, and Chandos went in search of the men of the Great Company, who came to him; and how several other Englishmen left the bastard Enrique and came from Spain to the prince; and when the Bastard heard this, he wished he had prevented the English, and tried to cut off the roads so that they could not reach the prince.*

The prince returned to Bordeaux and got his men ready. He sent for many noble and valiant knights from all over his lands, leaving out neither great nor small; nor did Chandos stay idle, because he went to fetch men of the Great Company, as many as fourteen squadrons, not counting those who returned from Spain when they heard that the prince was going to the aid of king Pedro. They took leave of king Enrique, who let them go and paid them well, for he no longer needed them. He was then king of Castile, and was well content, because he did not think anyone could overthrow him, since his power was so great. Those who came back were Eustace d'Abrichecourt, Devereux, Cresswell, Briquet, the lord of Aubeterre and Bernard de la Salle; in fact, all the prince's companions returned to Aquitaine, but not without difficulty, because as soon as the Bastard learnt that the prince was hastening to the aid of king Pedro, he did his best to prevent them; he cut off the roads and every morning and evening laid ambushes for them, and got men at arms riding mules and other ruffians to attack them. But the Lord God brought them to the safety of the prince's lands, which pleased the prince greatly, because he was very keen to achieve his plan. And then he gathered gold, silver and coin to pay his men.

All this took place three weeks before Christmas in the year 1366.

*Of the great preparations made by the prince at Bordeaux for his expedition to Spain.*

The noble prince ordered payments on a generous scale. Then the armourers at Bordeaux forged swords and daggers, coats of mail, helms, short swords, axes, gauntlets, in such number that it would have done for thirty kings.

*How the army gathered at Dax, and the companies camped in the Basque country and in the mountains for more than two months waiting to cross into Spain; and how they stayed there all winter, until February.*

The prince's army assembled at Dax, and all the barons and knights from the country around gathered there. All the companies encamped then in the Basque country, in the mountains, and waited for two months, with much hardship, until the passes were clear and they could set out on their expedition. They waited all winter, until February, until those from far off and nearby had all gathered.

*How the prince left Bordeaux and the noble lady the princess was bitterly unhappy at his departure; but the prince comforted her. Soon afterwards the princess gave birth to a son named Richard and the prince and many others were very pleased by this.*

But I have heard that the prince left Bordeaux a fortnight after Christmas; and then the noble princess was very sad at heart, and regretted that the goddess of love had paired her to such a noble prince, the most powerful alive in that century. She said again and again: 'Alas, gods and loves, what shall I do if I lose the true flower of all gentleness, the flower of all nobility, he who has no peer in the world for courage? Death, you would be near to me then. Now my heart and blood and veins fail me when I think of his departure, because everyone says that so dangerous an expedition has never been undertaken. Sweet Father of Heaven, comfort me with Your mercy.' When the prince heard this, he comforted her nobly, and told her: 'Lady, stop weeping and do not distress yourself, for God has power over everything.' The prince sweetly comforted his lady, and then took his leave of her, saying lovingly: 'Lady, we shall see each other again, and will celebrate together, we and all our friends, I am sure of it.' They embraced each other and kissed goodbye, while ladies and girls wept for their husbands and lovers. The princess's grief was all the greater because she was expecting a child; and in her grief she gave birth to a son, who was called Richard. Everyone was delighted at this, and the prince as well was very pleased: everyone said, 'This is a good beginning.'

*How the prince left Bordeaux and came to Dax and stayed there until he heard that his brother the duke of Lancaster was coming to him and then waited while the duke hastened to the prince, riding through Cotentin and Brittany where duke John welcomed him in noble style.*

Then the prince departed, and did not wait or stay there any longer. He came to Dax and stayed there, because news was brought to him that the duke of Lancaster was coming, with a large body of men. So he decided to stay and wait for his brother. When the noble duke heard that the prince had left Bordeaux, he was very sad, because he was afraid that he would not reach him in time. The duke landed in Cotentin, and hastened on his way with all his noble knights. From Cotentin he went to Brittany, and a fine company came to meet him, John, duke of Brittany and all the greatest barons of the country, his greatest friends, Clisson, Knolles and many others, who did him great honour. He welcomed the duke to his country, but the duke did not stay long, for he had to hurry to join the prince, who wanted to cross the mountains. So he took his leave of duke John and his wife without delay.

*How the duke of Lancaster rode as far as Bordeaux, when he found the princess who made him welcome and asked him for news from England; and after that the duke of Lancaster rode through the Landes to Dax, where he found his brother the prince, who came to meet him; and they met in friendly fashion: the prince asked him for news from England, and they were pleased to be together, and the count of Foix was there too.*

The noble duke of Lancaster rode day and night until he came to Bordeaux; and there he found the princess, mistress of all honour, who made him welcome, and asked him for news of her own country, what was happening in England; and the duke told her. And then he hardly waited before leaving Bordeaux: he rode across the Landes and hastened to the city of Dax. He found the prince his brother, who came to meet him with more than twenty knights, and the count of Foix was there as well. They were very pleased to see each other, and kissed as soon as they met; and the prince said, smiling: 'Duke of Lancaster, my brother, welcome to our land. Tell me, how are the king and queen and our brothers and friends?' 'Sire,' he said, 'thanks be to God, they are all well. Our father says that if he can do anything, send word to him. Our mother sends you greetings. All our brothers ask to be remembered to you, and say that they would gladly have come if they had been given leave.'

*How the duke of Lancaster and the prince came to Dax in great joy and waited to cross the passes, namely the pass of Roncevaux; and how the count of Foix returned home, and it was said that the king of Navarre was allied to the bastard Enrique and Sir Hugh Calveley had taken some towns in Navarre; and the king of Navarre sent word of this to the prince. Afterwards Sir Martin came from Navarre to the prince and helped them to cross.*

So they came to Dax, talking and holding hands, and there was much rejoicing that night. What they spoke of I do not know and cannot tell you. The count of Foix returned to his own country, and the prince remained at Dax, awaiting the moment when he could cross the passes. He did not yet know if he could cross by the pass of Roncevaux, because it was said that the king of Navarre had allied himself to the bastard Enrique, which caused much dismay. But at the same time Hugh de Calveley had taken Miranda and Puente la Reina, which had frightened the men of Navarre. The king sent his messenger straight to the prince to tell him what Hugh had done. After this Sir Martin came from Navarre, who by his wise advice helped them to cross.

*How the king of Navarre came to the prince at St Jean Pied-du-Port and the duke of Lancaster went to meet him and the oaths were renewed there; after that the vanguard was ordered to cross.*

Soon after this the king of Navarre came to St Jean Pied-du-Port, and the duke of Lancaster and Chandos went to meet him. They led him to the prince, whom they found at a place called Peyrehorade. King Pedro came as well and their oaths were renewed on the Host, and they all agreed what they should have. The king and the duke and Chandos left the next day for it was agreed that the vanguard should pass first, the following Monday. They soon arrived at St Jean and lodged there; and the next day it was proclaimed that everyone chosen for the vanguard was to be ready to cross the following Monday.

*How the duke of Lancaster led the vanguard, and which lords and others were in his company.*

Now I will tell you who was in the vanguard. Firstly, there was the duke of Lancaster, and there were many noble knights accompanying him: Thomas Ufford, Hugh Hastings, William Beauchamp, son of the earl of Warwick, and the lord of Neufville with many noble knights whom I will speak of elsewhere. Then there was Chandos, constable of the army; I will tell you his companions' names: the lord of Retz, the lord of Aubeterre, Garsiot du Chastel, Gilbert de la Motte, Aimery de Rochechouart, Sir Robert Camyn, Cresswell, Briquet, William Felton, William le Boteller, Peverell, John Sandes, John Alein, Shakill and Hawley. All these bannerets were with Chandos, and placed under his pennon. Then came the marshals, Stephen Cosyngton and Guichard d'Angle: with them they had the banner of St George and many other knights.

*How the vanguard of ten thousand horse crossed the pass and with great difficulty and hardship encamped in Navarre.*

Now I have told you all about the vanguard: they did not delay, but all crossed on Monday 14 February; but since God died for us on the cross there was never such a difficult crossing, for you could see men and horses stumbling on the mountainside because they were so hard pressed. No-one stopped for his companion, not even a father for his son. There was such great cold, snow and frost there, that everyone was afraid; but by God's mercy, all of them crossed, more than ten thousand horses and men, and encamped in Navarre. The next day, all those who were in the prince's battalion got ready to cross.

*Of the lords who were with the prince in his battalion and others, twenty thousand horse in all, and how they crossed the pass, led by the king of Navarre.*

Firstly, there were the prince and king Pedro and the king of Navarre; then Louis d'Harcourt, Eustace d'Abrechicourt, Thomas Felton, the lord of Parthenay and all the Pommiers brothers, who were noble knights, and the lord of Clisson and lord of Curton. The lord de la Warre, and Sir Robert Knollys, the Viscount of Rochechouart, the lord of Bourchier with many honourable knights, the seneschals of Aquitaine, Poitou, Angoumois, Saintonge, Périgord and Quercy, and the grand seneschal of Bigorre: all these were in the prince's battalion, with more than four thousand others, whom I shall not list. Almost twenty thousand horses crossed on the Tuesday; and the king of Navarre went with the prince and led him to the other side. And God, who is merciful, let them pass, but the noble prince of Aquitaine suffered much hardship in the journey.

*How the king of Majorca, the count of Armagnac and many other valiant lords and knights in the rearguard crossed the pass and encamped near Pamplona.*

On the Wednesday the rearguard passed as well, the noble king of Majorca and the valiant count of Armagnac, Bérard d'Albret, the lord of Mussidan and other honourable knights of renown; other pennons were carried by Sir Bertrucat d'Albret, the bastard of Breteuil and the bastard Camus, Naudon de Bageran, Bernard de la Salle and Lamy. All these were in the rearguard, and crossed on Wednesday. All of them encamped near Pamplona, where they found wine and bread enough for all to eat their fill.

*How the sire d'Albret and the Captal and two hundred men at arms crossed, and the whole army reassembled and the bastard Enrique heard of it.*

Not long afterwards the noble lord d'Albret crossed, and with him the captal, each with two hundred fighting men, brave men at arms; so the whole army was assembled. News of it was brought to Enrique, the bastard of Spain, who was staying at Santo Domingo with his followers. He was not particularly frightened, but decided, on the advice of his council, to send a letter at once to the prince.

*How the bastard Enrique sent letters to the prince to learn where he wished to enter Spain and to say that he would give battle to him.*

The letter read: 'To the most powerful, honoured and noble prince of Aquitaine. Sire, it is common knowledge, as we have heard, that you and your men have crossed the passes and are in alliance with our enemy. We are very surprised at this, and I do not know who has advised you, because we never did any injury to you nor undertook anything which would have given you cause to hate us, or to take from us the little land that God has given us; but as we know that no earthly lord in this world nor other creature has been granted such success in war as you, and that you and your men have come to seek battle, we ask you to be so kind as to tell us where you will enter our lands: for we hereby warn you that we shall be there to give battle.' Then he had the letters sealed, and sent them by his herald, who rode until he came to the prince, and gave them to him.

*How the prince received the Bastard's letters and showed them to king Pedro, and called a council of his barons to answer the letters; and how at that time Sir Thomas Felton asked, and was given, leave to seek out the Bastard's army. He rode off with a group of knights, squires and archers, crossed the river at Logroño and encamped at Navarete. At the same time the king of Navarre was treacherously captured; Martin de La Carra was made governor of Navarre, and brought the news to the prince, begging him to guard and govern the country. The prince promised to help him. Then the prince ordered the army to be ready to move off the next day; they crossed the pass of Arruazu, and rode through Guipuzcoa to Salvatierra.*

The prince was very pleased with this letter, and showed it to his barons, and explained it to them. Then he sent for king Pedro and summoned all his councillors to advise him how to reply. But at that time Sir Thomas Felton asked the prince a favour, that he should be granted leave to ride out and seek out the position of the enemy army. The prince agreed, and Thomas named the companions he wished to have: Thomas Ufford, William Felton, Hugh Stafford, Knollys, and Simon Burley as well. There were twenty lances and three hundred archers. They rode off through Navarre, travelling day and night. At Logroño they crossed the river, a fast and furious stream, and encamped at Navarete. While they were doing this, the king of Navarre was treacherously taken, which astonished the prince and his council. Martin de La Carra was made governor and keeper of Navarre on the queen's advice, and came to the prince, telling him how the king was captured and begging him to protect and govern the country. The prince was very surprised by what he had to say, and answered: 'I am very sorry that the king has been captured. I cannot go to free him now, but you know that the best I can do for him is to leave his lands: and if this does any good, may it be for him as much as for me: otherwise, I do not know what to advise.' Then he ordered the army to be ready as soon as it was daylight, asking Martin to provide guides, which he did. They went through the pass of Arruazu, a narrow little place, where the army suffered much hardship, and rode across Guipuzcoa: but he found little in the way of provisions for his army anywhere until he came to Salvatierra.

*How the prince and his army entered Spain and encamped in villages near Salvatierra, and wanted to take the town by storm, but it surrendered to king Pedro. The prince spent six days there, while his men were at Navarete. The latter found the Bastard's army and they captured the knight on watch, who was taken by Simon Burley; and two or three others were captured, who gave them information about the Bastard's army. They sent news of this to the prince.*

So the army entered Spain, and spread out across the country. The lords encamped in the villages near Salvatierra, and wanted to storm the town, but it surrendered to king Pedro as soon as he was seen there. The prince spent six days in the country around Salvatierra, while his men were at Navarete: they rode out often, and spied on the Bastard's army. One night they attacked the watch, hurling themselves on them on horseback, and took the knight of the watch and two or three others before the alarm was raised. The knight was taken prisoner by Simon Burley. Then they returned in haste to their camp at Navarete; they learned the truth about the army from the prisoners they had taken and sent word at once to the prince.

*How the Bastard moved off and came to meet the prince, and Thomas Felton and his companions left Navarete, riding in front of the Bastard's army to see more clearly what they were doing. They came to Vittoria and sent news to the prince; so the prince came near to Vittoria, as did the Bastard. He encamped on the slope of a mountain, while the prince stayed in the fields, where he met his knights and welcomed them.*

The Bastard heard news of the other army, and said that he would move off to meet them. And Thomas Felton and his companions knew of this and left Navarete, riding all the time in front of the army so that they could report on its movements. They stayed on the other side until the Spaniards had crossed and it was clear that they were going to Vittoria, on this side of the mountains. Sir Thomas Felton and his companions encamped on the plain in front of Vittoria, and sent to the prince to tell him what they had done. When the prince heard how things stood, and that the Bastard was coming to him to give battle, he said: 'By our Lord, the Bastard is bold! Let us go to meet him and take up our positions in front of Vittoria.' The next day he came to Vittoria, but the Bastard was not yet in sight, because he was on the plain on the other side of the mountain. When the prince reached the fields there, he found his knights there. He was very pleased to see them, and said: 'Lords, you are welcome, a hundred times welcome!'

*How the prince's outriders reported the enemy's movements, and the prince arrayed his men and divided them into battalions under different banners; and how several lords and others were knighted.*

As they were talking, the prince's outriders came in from the fields and reported that they had seen the enemy outriders. Then there was a stir throughout the army and soon they all gathered, with cries of 'To arms!' The prince drew up his men, and set his battalions in order. There you could see – a sight to make a bystander rejoice – fine gold, azure and silver, gules and sable, sinaple, purple and ermine; there were many precious banners of silk and sendal, for such a fine sight has never been seen since. The vanguard was drawn up in splendid array that day, and noble squires were knighted. The prince knighted king Pedro first of all, then Thomas Holland, Hugh, Philip and Peter Courtenay; John Trivet and Nicholas Bond. The duke knighted Ralph Camoys, Walter Ursewick, Thomas d'Auvirmetri and John Grendon; he made twelve or so knights in all. But there were also many good men knighted whose names I do not know, but I have heard it said that the prince and his men made more than two hundred knights that day.

*How the prince's army was drawn up to await battle, but the enemy did not appear that day because his rearguard was seven leagues behind. At vespers the prince's host encamped, and it was proclaimed that everyone was to return to the plain the next day ready for action.*

They stood in order, ready for the attack, all that day. But it did not please our Lord that the enemy should come that day, because the rearguard was more than seven leagues of the country behind;★ and the prince was very angry at this. At vespers they returned to their camp. The prince had a proclamation made that everyone was to go back to the plain, and no-one was to go beyond the vanguard; everyone was to remain on guard and encamp with his banner-

★ It is not clear whether this refers to the Spaniards or English, though the compiler of the introductory paragraph takes it to refer to the English.

company. But Sir Thomas and William Felton went and encamped more than two leagues away.

*How count Tello, brother of the Bastard, asked leave to ride out and spy on the prince's army; he was given leave, and rode off with several lords and others, six thousand in all.*

Now I will tell you about don Tello, the noble count, who said to his brother, the Bastard Enrique: 'Sire, listen to me. It is obvious that the enemy are encamped near here. If you wish, and will give me leave, I will ride off at dawn and report on what the enemy are doing.' The Bastard at once replied that he would agree to this and that his brother Sancho and the marshal d'Audenham should go with him. The raiding party was to be made up of six thousand men. Sir Bertrand du Guesclin would have gone on it; but he only arrived from Aragon that day, or so I am told. They spoke menacingly against the English, saying that they should die a shameful death for their outrage.

*How the count don Tello and his men approached the prince's army, meeting first Sir Hugh Calveley, and how they would have surprised the vanguard if it had not been for the duke of Lancaster.*

The prince was encamped outside Vittoria, and every house and hovel was full of his men. But the prince was not aware on the next day of the raid which don Tello was preparing: for the latter rose at midnight and rode along a broad highway up the mountain and down a valley. The first person he met was Hugh Calveley who was leaving his encampment and coming to the prince. The raiders did great damage to his packhorses and waggons, and much noise was made about it: they rode up and down the lodgings, and many were killed in their beds. The vanguard would have been completely taken by surprise if it had not been for the duke of Lancaster. As soon as he heard the shouts, he left his lodging and went out on the hillside, where he assembled his company and the others, as best he could. The Spaniards intended to take the hillside, but all the banners of the army gathered round the duke's banner; the prince and Chandos arrived, and the army was drawn up in order. The raiders were driven off, everyone doing his part.

# The Campaigns of the Black Prince

*How the large battalion of Spaniards rode on until they came across William Felton and several other knights on a hillside, and how William Felton hurled himself on the enemy like a brave knight, and killed a Spaniard in knightly fashion. He fought bravely, but the enemy hurled lances and javelins at him until his horse was killed under him, and in the end he was killed.*

Meanwhile the large battalion of Spaniards rode on and met Felton, Richard Taunton, Degory Says, Ralph Hastings, Gaillard Beguer and many good and valiant knights: there were a hundred fighting men there, both great and small. They gathered their company on a little hillside; but Sir William boldly and bravely threw himself on horseback into the enemy like a madman, his lance in rest. He charged down and struck a Spaniard on his flowered shield, and made him feel his keen steel blade right through his heart, hurling him to the earth before everyone's eyes. He went for them with drawn sword, and the Castilian forces followed him on all sides, throwing lances and javelins at him. They killed his horse under him, but Sir William Felton defended himself fiercely on foot; though it was little use, for he was killed in the end. God have mercy on him!

*How about six thousand Spaniards launched a heavy attack on the English on the hillside, who were not more than a hundred; and the English fought bravely. But in the end they were taken and led to the bastard Enrique.*

And the others gathered on a hillside, which they seized; there the Spaniards launched many attacks on them, pressing them hard and hurling javelins and lances and spears at them. And that brave band of men proved their courage that day, because they charged down more than a hundred times with drawn swords and made them retreat, nor could the Castilians harm them by throwing lances and darts; but the Bretons, Normans, Picards and Burgundians came up the valley, led by marshal d'Audrehem, and Sir Jean de Neufville: they were a thousand in all. As soon as they saw them, they all dismounted: both English and Gascons saw that they could not hold out much longer, for no help was in sight and the French came on at the double to attack them. They defended themselves relentlessly, but they were only a hundred against six thousand, and though they did unsurpassed deeds of arms, to match those of Roland and Oliver, their defence was little use, because they had to yield as prisoners. Hastings and Degory Says were taken there, Gaillard Beguer, the three Felton brothers, Richard Taunton, Mytton and a number of others who I will not name. The prince was very sad at this; but he thought that the whole of the enemy army had come down through the pass, so he did not want to break up his army; if it had not been for this he would have gone to help his other men, as he should have done. But the enemy, when they had finished, learnt that the prince was nearby, and left as soon as they could, to return to their own army. They took the prisoners with them, guarding them closely.

*How the Bastard was delighted at count Tello's return and at the capture of the English, and threatened the prince and his men; and what he was advised to do to destroy the English; meanwhile the prince and his men were at Vittoria awaiting battle.*

On their return, king Enrique made much of them, saying, 'Welcome, lords, you have done well.' He went on: 'All the others will go the same way. The prince thinks he will attack me and take my lands; I will show him that it is greed for money that has made him undertake this expedition. I will give anyone who can take him prisoner a wealth of gold and silver.' When the marshal heard him, he said gently to him: 'Sire, what are you saying? You have not defeated all the enemy knights yet. But you can be sure that when you fight them you will find they are good men at arms. But if you will listen to good advice, you can deal with them without striking a blow. Make sure the pass by which they want to come through is safely held, and keep your army under control. If you do not fight a battle, you will see them leave Spain for lack of provisions, or else die of hunger.' This was the advice of the French to the Bastard. Meanwhile the prince's army was still drawn up on the fields outside Vittoria, for he continued to wait and see whether the Bastard would come down in battle order, with his banners unfurled. That night he camped in the fields, and his men were none too pleased, because many had neither bread nor wine. It was no easy rest, because there were frequent attacks and skirmishes, and some of the English and of the enemy were killed. The weather, too, was vile, with rain and wind.

*Of the weather at this time; how the prince decamped and rode through Navarre, crossed the Paso de la Guardia and came to Viana; there he stayed, and afterwards crossed the bridge at Logroño, and encamped in the orchards near Logroño. The Bastard returned from San Vicente and encamped on the river before Najera; and how the prince sent a letter to the Bastard.*

All this took place in March, when there is often wind, snow and rain – there was never worse weather – and the prince was in the fields, where men and horses suffered badly. On the Monday the prince decamped and rode back through Navarre, through a pass called the Paso de la Guardia; he rode on until he came to Viana and camped there. Soon after this he crossed the bridge at Logroño. The prince, who was very anxious for a battle, camped in the orchards and olive groves around Logroño. And the spies of the Bastard told him that the Prince was encamped in the gardens there. Then he did not delay for an evening or a morning, but turned back from San Vicente, and encamped by the river near Najera in a vineyard; he had a powerful and noble army with him.

*How the prince sent the Bastard letters, as follows.*

Then the prince sent the Bastard a letter, saying: 'To the noble and honoured Enrique, duke of Trastamare, at present calling himself king of Castile. We have read the news contained in your present letter, which is gracious and gentle, and in which you say that you would very much like to know why we have allied and pledged ourselves to your enemy, whom we regard as our friend. We say that we are obliged to do so by alliances made in the past, and out of friendship, and in order to uphold justice. For you must surely know in your heart that it is not right for a bastard to be king and disinherit the rightful heir; no man born of a lawful marriage can agree to that. We must also enlighten you on another point: as you are so esteemed and brave, we would like to bring about a reconciliation between the two of you. I would be glad to try to do this, and for my part would try to obtain a great estate for you in Castile. But it is reasonable and right that you should abandon your claim to the crown, so that peace can be made between us. As far as entering Spain is concerned, with God's help I and my companions will enter where we please, without asking leave.'

*How a herald took the prince's letters to the Bastard, and the Bastard asked his council for their advice; which each of them gave, and they made their plans against the prince accordingly.*

So the letter was dictated and sealed. It was given to a herald, who was delighted by it, because he was also given jewels, ermine robes and furred mantles. He took his leave without further delay and went to his master, king Enrique, to whom he gave the letter. When the Bastard read it and learnt what the prince intended, he knew he had a brave opponent. He summoned his council, and asked: 'What do you think would be the best course?' Everyone said what he thought. Sir Bertrand du Guesclin told him: 'Sire, have no fear; you will soon fight a battle. You little know how great a force the prince is leading; he has with him the flower of chivalry and knighthood, the best fighting men in the world. You need to equip your men and organise them.' 'Sir Bertrand, do not be afraid,' replied the Bastard Enrique, 'I shall have four thousand armed horse, which will be on the two wings of my battalion, and four thousand lightly armed horsemen, and two thousand of the best men at arms in all Spain. I can also have fifty thousand footsoldiers and six thousand crossbowmen. From here to Seville, there are neither free men nor serfs who are not ready to serve me; they have all sworn to regard me as their king, and I am not in the least frightened that I shall not have the better of this battle.' So they talked cheerfully and full of joy that night.

*How the prince decamped from Logroño the next morning, and his men rode two leagues that day, drawn up in battle order, thinking that there would be a battle that day; and he sent his outriders to report on the army of the Bastard Enrique which was encamped at Navarete; the two armies were then two leagues apart.*

The prince scarcely waited, but at dawn the next day decamped from in front of Logroño. He rode that morning in full battle order, and such an array of noble men has never been seen since our Saviour's birth. That day was the Friday. The prince rode two leagues that day without stopping, and thought that he would fight a battle that day. He sent out riders in all directions, who worked hard to find out what was happening; and they saw how the other army was drawn up, encamped on the river near Najera on the heath, in the orchards and in the fields – a mighty army indeed – and that they were doing nothing that showed they would ride out that day. They at once reported all this to the prince, how the army was encamped at Navarete, and told him how it was drawn up. So the two armies encamped two leagues apart. Everyone was on watch that night, ready to defend himself; they went to sleep in their armour. Before daylight king Enrique sent out spies to different parts of the English camp to find out how they were drawn up; but they moved off at dawn, and set out on horseback. The prince did not take the most direct route, but a road which led to the right. They rode up a hillside and down a valley in such noble array and close order that it was a marvel to see. The Bastard had not delayed either, but had already drawn up his battalion at midnight. Sir Bertrand and the marshal d'Audrehem were on foot, as well as count Sancho, and the count of Denia from Aragon; Le Bègue de Villaines was there, John de Neufville and more than four thousand others whose names I do not know, from Spain, Aragon, France, Picardy, Brittany, Normandy and many other distant countries. On the left was count Tello, on horseback, with more than twelve thousand light horse.

*Of the great battalion of the Bastard, who had fifteen thousand men at arms and many crossbowmen with him and four thousand one hundred armed horse; and the prior of the Hospitallers and the master of Santiago were in his battalion.*

On the right was the royal wing under Enrique, the bastard king, who had with him a good fifteen thousand men at arms and many men of the country – crossbowmen, villeins, servants, with lances and javelins and slings for throwing stones – as a guard for the front ranks. No-one had ever seen so many people as were gathered that day. There were many silk or sendal banners displayed. A little to one side were the armed horse, 4,100 in all. A very shrewd knight was in command, named Gomez Carrillo, with the prior of the Hospitallers, who said he would make the English suffer that day; there too were the master of Santiago and a bold knight called the master of Calatrava: he declared aloud that he would ride right through the enemy battalion that day.

*How the prince came down the hillside and Sir John Chandos was granted a banner, which delighted his companions; and they prepared to fight.*

Now everything was arranged and the army drawn up, and the prince wanted to set off down the hillside at once. When the two armies saw each other, they knew that there was no escape from a battle, and that it could not be delayed till the next day. Sir John Chandos came to the prince and brought him his rich silken banner. He said humbly to him: 'Sire, I have served you in the past, and all that God has given me has come through you. I am, and always will be, your man. And if it seems the right time and place for me to have a banner, I can well support that rank from what God has provided. Now do as you wish: here is the banner, and I present it to you.' Then the prince, king Pedro and the duke of Lancaster unfurled the banner, and gave it to him by the shaft, saying: 'God grant that you may do nobly with it.' So Chandos took his banner and set it up among his comrades, saying: 'Sirs, here is my banner, guard it as if it were your own, for it is yours as much as mine.' His companions were delighted by this. Then they continued on their way, not wanting to wait any longer for the battle; and the banner was carried by William Alby.

*How the English dismounted and the prince prayed to God Almighty and spoke privately to king Pedro; then the vanguard advanced.*

The English, eager to win honour, now dismounted. The prince spoke to them: 'Lords, we have no other course. You know that we are near to starvation for want of provisions; look at our enemies over there, who have enough food, bread, wine and salt and fresh-fish of all kinds. But we must conquer them with our swords. Let us do such deeds today that we may depart with honour.' Then the prince joined his hands in prayer, saying: 'Sovereign Father who didst create us, Thou knowest truly that I have only come here to sustain right, bravery and nobility, all of which urge me to win a life of honour; therefore I pray You to keep myself and my men safely.' And when the prince had prayed, he said: 'Banners, forward! God is with our cause!' Then the prince took king Pedro aside and said to him: 'Today you will know for certain if you will recapture Castile. Trust in God!' This was what the prince told him.

*How the duke of Lancaster and Sir John Chandos went in the vanguard, and knights were made there; and the duke encouraged his men.*

In the vanguard was the noble duke of Lancaster; and the good knight Chandos knighted many men there: Curzon, Prior, Elton, William Ferindon, Aimery de Rochechouart, Gaillard de la Motte and Robert Briquet. Many knights were made there, full of valour and of noble and powerful descent. On the field, the duke of Lancaster said to William Beauchamp: 'Look, there are our enemies; but, may Christ help me, you will see that I am a good knight today, if death does not prevent me.' Then he said: 'Banners, forward, forward! Let us take the Lord God as our protector, and let every man acquit himself honourably.' Then the brave duke put himself at the head of his men, which made many of them even more bold and brave. At this time the duke knighted Jean d'Ypres.

*How the great battle began, and of the lords who were with the duke of Lancaster's battalion; how Sir Bertrand joined battle and many good knights were thrown to the ground.*

Now the battle began and the dust began to rise. The archers fired volleys thicker than rain ever fell. The duke of Lancaster went out in front like a brave man, followed by Thomas Ufford and Hugh Hastings, each with their banner unfurled and lance couched. On the right was Chandos, who won great fame that day, Stephen Cosyngton, John Devereux, Guichard d'Angle, who had his two sons with him, and other worthy knights who did their duty well; and the lord de Retz was also there. You could see the company approach, closely grouped, with banners and pennons unfurled: they all held their lances couched and were eager to attack the enemy. All the time the archers fired and the crossbowmen of the Bastard's army returned their fire. But they continued on foot until they met Sir Bertrand's battalion, who put up a stout resistance. When they met, swords clashed and everyone strove to do his best. No-one in the world was so bold of heart that he would not have been frightened by the great blows they gave each other with their battleaxes, swords and daggers. It was no party, for many good knights were thrown to the ground.

*How many banners were hurled to the ground and Sir John Chandos was beaten down; a Castilian fell on him and wounded him but by the grace of God he recovered and killed the Castilian, and afterwards rejoined the mêlée and fought strongly.*

There was much noise and clouds of dust. There was hardly a banner or pennant which was not hurled to the ground. At one point that day Chandos was beaten down; a tall Castilian fell on him – Martín Fernandez was his name – who tried hard to kill him, and wounded him through his visor. Chandos boldly took a dagger from his belt and struck the Castilian, burying the sharp weapon in his body. The Castilian stretched himself out, dead, and Chandos got to his feet. He took his sword in hand and plunged into the mêlée again, which was very fierce and fearful and amazing to watch. Whoever he struck was sure to be killed.

*How the duke of Lancaster fought in knightly fashion and put himself in the greatest danger.*

And elsewhere the noble duke of Lancaster fought so hard that everyone was amazed, watching his great prowess and how he proudly put himself into danger; I do not think that anyone, rich or poor, pushed forward as he did that day. And the prince did not linger, but came on to attack at more than walking pace.

*How the king of Navarre's standard bearer and Sir Martin de La Carra set out with the captal de Buch and two thousand men to attack count don Tello; but before they could attack, don Tello fled.*

On the right of the battle, the king of Navarre's standard-bearer and Sir Martin de La Carra set out with the captal and the sire d'Albret – they were two thousand strong – to attack don Tello, who was to the left of Sir Bertrand; but I can assure you that before they could come to grips with don Tello he began to withdraw, and the captal turned back at once to attack the footsoldiers. They gave them much work that day: as brave men should, they defended themselves valiantly. On the left, on the other side of the prince, Percy, the lord de Clisson, Sir Thomas Felton and Sir Walter Hewitt visited the vanguard and encouraged them.

*How the prince joined battle with his great battalion and how the rearguard was ordered to station itself on a little hill facing the armed horse; the king of Majorca and several other lords were there. The battle began on all sides and they fought until the Spaniards fled.*

Then the fighting grew fiercer, and the slaughter increased, because the prince of Aquitaine led on all his great battalion. There was a little hill to the left; and the rearguard had been ordered to station itself there, to one side; the king of Majorca was there and the count of Armagnac, the lord of Severac, Sir Berard and Sir Bertrucat d'Albret; and Sir Hugh Calveley as well. The battle began on all sides, and it was fiercely fought. The Spaniards hurled javelins and lances, all doing their best, for the archers shot arrows thicker than winter rain. They wounded men and horses, and the Spaniards realised that they could not hold out any longer. They began to turn their horses and to take flight. When the Bastard Enrique saw this, he grew very angry and tried three times to rally them, saying, 'Lords, help me, because you made me king and swore to help me loyally.' But his words were useless, because the attack was continually renewed.

*How the Bastard fled and the Spanish were defeated; and the French fought next and were also defeated, Sir Bertrand and several lords and knights being captured and many men at arms killed. Of the English, lord Ferrers was killed in the battle.*

There was not a single man, however humble, in the prince's company, who was not as bold and brave as a lion: you could not compare them even to Roland and Oliver. The Spaniards turned and fled, all giving their horses their heads. The Bastard was sad and furious when he saw them; but they had to flee if they were not to be captured or killed. Then the slaughter began, and you could see footsoldiers being killed with daggers and swords. The Bastard fled along a valley. But the French, Bretons and Normans were still in position, though their morale lasted only a little while, for they were soon defeated: everywhere there were shouts of 'Guyenne! St George!'. Sir Bertrand and the marshal d'Audrehem were captured there, and a very valiant count, the count of Denia. The count Sanchez, one of the enemy captains, was taken, with Le Bègue de Villaines, Sir Jean de Neufville and two thousand others. Le Bègue de Villiers was killed, and many others whose names I do not know. But according to reports five hundred or more men at arms died there in hand-to-hand fighting. On the English side, an excellent knight died, the lord Ferrers. May God and St Peter have mercy on his soul!

*The scene of the great battle, and the pursuit afterwards; how more than two thousand Spaniards were drowned in a river and about seven thousand seven hundred killed, so that the water ran crimson. The English entered the town and took prisoners. The prince, who stayed by his standard, was delighted by this.*

The site of the battle was a pleasant plain, without a tree or bush for a league around, beside a fine river, very swift and strong; and this river caused much harm to the Castilians that day, for the pursuit continued as far as the river. More than two thousand drowned there. On the bridge in front of Najera the pursuit was very fierce; you could see knights leaping into the water for fear, and dying one on top of each other. And the river ran crimson, to everyone's amazement, with the blood of dead men and horses. There was such slaughter there that I do not think that anyone ever saw anything like it; the dead were so many that the total came to seven thousand seven hundred. The prince's men entered the town, and more than a thousand were killed there. The Grand Master of Calatrava was captured in a cellar; the prior of the Hospitallers and the master of Santiago were also taken. They had retreated behind a high wall, but this did not protect them, for men at arms climbed over it and were preparing to attack them when they humbly yielded rather than face them. So the Spaniards were killed and taken, much to the joy of the prince, who waited on the battlefield, his standard raised, to rally his men. This battle took place on a Saturday, three days into the month of April; that was the date of the great battle at Najera.

*How the prince stayed that night where the Bastard and his men had stayed the night before; how they celebrated and thanked God, and found plenty of food and great riches.*

That night the prince stayed in the very lodging where king Enrique had spent the previous night. They celebrated the victory, and thanked God the Father, the Son and His blessed Mother for the favour shown to them; and they found bread and wine there – the house was full of it – and chests, plate, gold and silver, which pleased many of them.

*How king Pedro came to the prince and thanked him for what he had done for him; and how he told the prince that he wanted to be revenged on his enemies; and of the prince's reply and his wise advice.*

King Pedro came to the prince, who was very cheerful, and said to him: 'My dear cousin, I must thank you, for today you have done so much for me that I can never repay it in my lifetime.' 'Sire,' he answered, 'as you please, but thank God and not me, for by my faith God has done it and not I, and both of us should be ready to thank Him for it.' Don Pedro said that he spoke the truth, and he was pleased by this, but he wished to take his revenge on the traitors who had forcibly caused him such harm.

*How the prince advised king Pedro to pardon those who had opposed him and king Pedro granted him this, except for a man named Gomez Carrillo, who was drawn through the army, and his throat was cut.*

Then the prince said to him: 'Sire, grant me one thing, I ask you, if you can agree.' King Pedro said: 'Why do you ask me? Everything I have is yours.' The prince quickly said: 'Sire, I want nothing that is yours. But I advise you that if you want to be king of Castile, you should send word everywhere that you have granted one thing: pardon to all your enemies. And if by bad advice and ill will anyone has supported king Enrique, pardon them at once, provided that they come willingly to ask for mercy.' King Pedro agreed to grant this, but he was very loath to do it. He said to the prince of Aquitaine 'Cousin, I grant you this, with one exception; I would not take all the gold in Seville to spare Gomez Carrillo, for he is the traitor who has done me most harm.' The prince said: 'Do as you like with him, and pardon the rest.' His brother the Bastard was brought and many other prisoners, whom he freely pardoned on account of the prince's request. Then he returned to his lodging, and Gomez Carrillo was brought there, and dragged through the army and his throat was cut in front of everyone.

*How the prince and king Pedro left Najera and went to Burgos, and the news spread everywhere.*

The next Monday, the prince left Najera with king Pedro. They rode to Burgos, and the news of the Bastard's defeat spread throughout Spain.

*How the Bastard's wife was at Burgos; when she heard the news, she fled in sorrow to Aragon, complaining bitterly of her fate and praising the prince. And the prince lodged at Briviesca.*

The Bastard's wife was at Burgos, and she had no time to waste. As soon as she learned the news, she left as quickly as she could, taking everything that she could carry with her. She rode day and night with her escort until she reached Aragon. She was very distressed, crying and weeping, and saying: 'Why was I born? I was queen of Castile, with a golden crown, but my good luck has lasted no time at all. Death, who comes to everyone, why are you waiting? I want to die, for I shall never find relief or happiness while men can say "Look at the queen of Spain who was given the crown by the Great Company." Prince, it is your great power that has deposed me. The lady who is married to you has high honour indeed, because she can say that she has the flower of the world, its best knight, and the ruler of everyone.' So the lady said, bemoaning her fate. Meanwhile, the noble prince halted at Briviesca, and king Pedro rode on to Burgos.

*How king Pedro rode to Burgos and the men of Burgos came to meet him and welcomed him; after which the prince came to Burgos and stayed there for a month; king Pedro sent messengers throughout Spain, and people came from all parts to ask for pardon, and he pardoned them.*

The rich citizens of the town came to meet him, saying 'Welcome, king!' So he was received at Burgos, and the prince came six days later: he stayed there for a good month. Messengers were sent everywhere in Spain, to every city and town, to Toledo, Seville, Cordoba and León, to all parts of the kingdom, to tell people to come at once to beg mercy from king Pedro. So strangers and well-known men came from everywhere, and the king pardoned them all.

*How the prince held judgement outside Burgos and all Spain was at his command; and Fernandez de Castres came, whom the prince honoured greatly, and gave a noble welcome; and the prince stayed there more than seven months, and the oaths were renewed.*

The prince held judgement outside Burgos and held gage of battle;* you could have said that his power in Spain was such that everything was done as he commanded. Fernandez de Castres came, and the prince welcomed him and did him great honour. The prince

* Perhaps meaning that he offered to defend Pedro's right to the throne against all challengers.

and his barons stayed at the rich city of Burgos for seven months or more, holding council there; and the oaths which they had sworn were renewed.

*How king Pedro went to Seville to buy silver and gold to pay the prince and his men; the prince waited for him at Valladolid for six months and his men suffered great hardship for want of food.*

It was agreed that king Pedro should go to Seville to buy silver and gold to pay the prince and his men; the prince would await king Pedro at Valladolid and the country around, and a day was fixed for his return. But in fact the prince waited six months for him, and his army suffered great hardship, hunger and thirst, for lack of wine and bread. I have heard a proverb which says that you should argue for your wife but fight for your food. There is no pleasure for anyone who has not eaten and drunk enough; and there were many men who did not eat bread every time they were hungry. But they did not dare attack towns or castles, because the prince had forbidden it. Yet even if they were hanged for it, they had to do it, so great was the famine. The prince himself took Amosco and then went to Medina del Campo, where he waited in the fields until the town gave him provisions; otherwise he would have attacked them. The Great Company, too, took several towns in Spain, but all the same they suffered hardships as they waited for king Pedro.

*How king Pedro sent letters to the prince, thanking him warmly and making excuses for not paying him; and the prince sent a letter back.*

When they had waited a long while, and it was past the day when he should have returned, he sent a letter to the prince, which said that he was most grateful for all his services, since he was king of all Castile, and everyone acknowledged him as lord; but his people had told him that he could have no money unless his army withdraw. So he begged the prince to return home, for there was nothing more for him to do, and to appoint men to receive the payment due. The prince was very surprised to hear this letter. He sent two knights to him with letters saying that he had not kept the oaths he had sworn.

*How the prince decided to return to Aquitaine because many said that the Bastard had entered his lands and was doing great damage; and the prince rode until he came to Val de Soria; and in the meanwhile Chandos conferred with the council of Aragon.*

The prince realised that king Pedro was not as true to his word as he had thought. So he said that he would return home, because many said that the Bastard Enrique had entered Aquitaine, and was making the common people of the country suffer much misery; and the prince was very angry at this. So the prince at once set out from Madrigal on his way home. He rode day and night until he came to the valley of Soria, where he stayed for a good month. Meanwhile Chandos conferred with the council of Aragon; but I know nothing of what they discussed.

*How Chandos and Sir Martin de La Carra came to the king of Navarre and obtained permission for the prince to pass; and the prince left the valley of Soria and went through Navarre; and the king of Navarre escorted him to the other side of the pass, where they parted; and the prince came to Bayonne, where he feasted for five days, and the citizens welcomed him.*

Chandos went quickly to the king of Navarre. He and Sir Martin de La Carra obtained leave from the king of Navarre for the prince to return across his lands. The prince did not delay, but left the valley of Soria, and, without halting, made his way across Navarre. The king did great honour to the prince, sending him great quantities of wine and food every day. He led him across Navarre, and took him to the other side of the pass. At St Jean Pied-du-Port they held a great feast, and then took their leave of each other. Then the prince came to Bayonne, which made many men glad. The citizens welcomed him nobly, as was right. He dismissed his men, and told them to come to Bordeaux for their payment. He spent five days feasting there.

*How the prince left Bayonne and came to Bordeaux, and was met by processions bearing crosses; and the princess and his son Edward came to meet him as well, with many ladies and knights, and they all rejoiced.*

The prince left Bayonne, and did not rest until he had reached Bordeaux. He was nobly received there, with processions bearing crosses, and all the clergy came to meet him. They welcomed him nobly, praising and thanking God. Then they went to the cathedral of St André. The princess came to meet him, and everyone rejoiced.

They embraced tenderly when they met: the prince kissed his wife and son, and went on foot to his lodging, holding them by the hand.

*How the prince stayed at Bordeaux amid great rejoicing, and how everyone in Aquitaine was glad of his return; and how his companions were welcomed by their friends.*

There were such rejoicings at Bordeaux that everyone was glad of the return of the prince and his companions, and everyone welcomed their friends. That night there was great joy throughout Aquitaine. So ends my account of the prince's great expedition with his nobles.

*How the prince, after he had stayed for a while at Bordeaux, assembled all his nobles at St Emilion, both those who had remained behind and those who had been with him in Spain; he welcomed them and gave them great gifts, and then each went to his lodging.*

He stayed for a while at Bordeaux, well satisfied with his people and country, because they had rejoiced at his return. Soon afterwards he gathered all the nobles of his principality, counts, barons, bishops and prelates: they came gladly. The prince courteously and humbly thanked them, both those who had been with him in Spain and those who had stayed behind to guard his lands. He said: 'Lords, I owe you my affection, for you have served me well. I thank you with all my heart.' He received them nobly, and gave them great gifts, gold, silver and rich jewels, and they were well pleased with them. They left the noble prince and went to their lodgings.

*How the prince came to Angoulême, and his illness began; and treachery and treason started among the lords of the country, because they agreed to make war on the prince.* (1367–8)

Soon after this, the prince of Aquitaine came to stay at Angoulême; and while he was there, the illness began which lasted for the rest of his life, which was a great pity. Then treachery and treason began to control the actions of those who should have loved him; for those he thought were his friends became his enemies; but that is not surprising, for the devil will always seek to harm a wise man rather than an evil-doer. As soon as it was known that the prince was ill and at death's door, his enemies decided to start the war again and began to negotiate with his enemies.

*How the war between France and England began again and towns, cities and many lords of the country turned against the prince and went to the king of France, appealing to him in court as their sovereign lord, saying that the prince had done them much wrong.* (1369)

Then the war between France and England began again, and then towns and cities changed sides, and many counts and barons as well, whose names I will not conceal: Armagnac, de L'Isle, Périgord, d'Albret, and Comminges, all renounced their allegiance to their lord the prince on the same day, because he was ill and could not look after his interests. They all agreed to appeal against the prince and start the war again. The count of Armagnac, with many knights, was the first to go to the king of France; and they told him that they wished to appeal to his court and return to his side, saying that the prince wronged and oppressed them: for that reason they had come to him as their sovereign lord.

*How the king of France summoned his great council and explained the count of Armagnac's intention; and the king of France sent a messenger to the prince requiring him to come and answer in his parliament, which made the prince very angry.*

The king of France summoned his great council, and told them the count of Armagnac's intentions, and how he was tempting him to start the war again. Then they conferred, and decided to summon the prince to come at once to answer the appeal in full parliament. The prince, who was ill, was very angry when he heard this. He lifted himself up in bed and said: 'Lords, I think, from what I hear, that the French believe I am dead; but if God gives me comfort and I can get up from this bed, I will cause them harm enough yet, because God knows that they complain of me now without good cause.'

*How the prince answered the king of France and the war began in Aquitaine.*

Then he replied boldly and freely to the king of France, that he would come at his command if God gave him health and life; he and all his company would be there, their helmets on their heads, to defend themselves from mischief. So the war began in Aquitaine, and men of the companies were put in all the garrisons. It was war to the death, very cruel in many places; brother fought brother, son fought father; each joined whichever side he pleased. But the prince lost much land, because there was treason and treachery on all sides. No-one could be trusted, but the prince took such comfort as he could nonetheless.

*How the prince sent to his father in England for help, and he sent Edmund, earl of Cambridge, his son and the earl of Pembroke, and many noble knights, who took Bourdeilles by assault; the earl of Pembroke was knighted, and then they besieged La Roche-sur-Yon.*

He sent to England for help and assistance, and the noble king his father sent his brother Edmund, earl of Cambridge, and the earl of Pembroke too; and they had many noble knights with them. These two went to the frontier, and did valuable work: they took Bourdeilles by assault, which heartened them, and the earl of Pembroke was knighted there. Soon after they besieged La Roche-sur-Yon; and Chandos was at Montauban, where he did good work.

*How La Roche-sur-Yon was taken by the earl of Cambridge and Audley and Chandos died.*

Fortune frowned horribly on the English in Aquitaine. La Roche-sur-Yon was taken by Cambridge and his men; but then it pleased God that Sir James Audley should die of sickness there; the prince was very sad at this, because James had been a close friend of his. Only a little while afterwards Chandos was killed at the bridge of Lussac, which much dismayed and grieved the prince. But when things go wrong, one misfortune often follows another; it often happens in this way. So all kinds of disasters came one after another and news of them came to the prince, who lay on his sickbed. But he praised God and said: 'Everything has its place; if I can get up again, I will take my revenge.'

*How the French rejoiced greatly at the prince's illness and the deaths of Chandos and Audley; and the king of France sent news of this to Bertrand du Guesclin in Spain, telling him to return; and he came back to Toulouse.*

When the French learned that Chandos was dead, they were very glad and rejoiced greatly, saying 'Everything will be ours again, as truly as the Paternoster.' Then Charles sent word without delay to Bertrand du Guesclin, who was in Spain, in the service of the Bastard, and told him that Chandos was dead. He was pleased to hear it. Bertrand scarcely waited at all before returning to France. He came to Toulouse, where the duke of Anjou was, who welcomed him nobly, and said to him as a friend: 'Sir Bertrand, welcome to you. We have great need of you, because if you are with us we shall conquer Aquitaine. Audley and Chandos, who did us so much damage, are dead, and the prince is lying in bed sick. So, if you think it a good idea, we are ready to raid his lands, and make war on him.'

*How Sir Bertrand agreed to make war on the prince, and the French gathered a great army; the duke of Anjou entered Quercy and the dukes of Berry and Bourbon rode through Limousin, intending to besiege the prince, when the prince got up from his sickbed and assembled his army. (1370)*

Sir Bertrand agreed to this plan and said that it was a good idea; and they all settled that they would mount a raid from two directions and besiege the prince. So they assembled their men in hundreds and thousands. The duke of Anjou rode through Quercy with a large following; the dukes of Berry and Bourbon with a great number of men rode through Limousin until they occupied Limoges. They intended, it seems, to go straight to besiege the prince, who was lying sick in bed at Angoulême. As soon as he heard this news, which seemed good to him, he got up and assembled all his forces.

*How the duke of Lancaster and many noble knights arrived in the country and wanted to go and fight the enemy; when the enemy learnt that the prince had gathered his army they retreated and did not dare await him. About then Limoges was surrendered treacherously; the prince besieged it and took it by assault, many men at arms and townsmen being killed.*

At this point the duke of Lancaster arrived in the country, with many noble knights, ready to fight the enemy in defence of those lands; but as soon as the enemy heard for certain that the prince had gathered his forces, they retreated and did not wait for him. But at the same time the good city of Limoges was surrendered by treachery, so the prince came there, and besieged it until he won it by assault; because Roger de Beaufort was there, who was sure that he could hold it, and Jean de Villemur and at least three hundred men at arms, as well as the citizens. But they were all killed or taken by the prince, much to the joy of all his friends; the enemy were very frightened and regretted that the war had started again.

*How after Limoges was taken the prince returned to Angoulême, where he found that Edward his eldest son had died, which grieved him greatly; and afterwards he came to England with his wife and his son Richard and many other of his men.*

After Limoges was taken, the valiant prince came back to Angoulême, where another evil omen occurred, for he found that his eldest son Edward had died, which grieved him greatly; but no-one can escape death, and he had to accept God's will. He scarcely waited to prepare for the voyage before leaving for England, because of the sickness that he was suffering from; and he took with him his wife and son and many noble knights.

*How the news came to England that La Rochelle was lost and the earl of Pembroke captured; at which the king of England assembled a very large army, including the prince and many famous knights; but they spent nine weeks at sea and the wind prevented them from crossing.* (1372)

After this came news that La Rochelle had been lost, and the earl of Pembroke captured. So the king gathered a great army; in it were all the most famous barons and knights. The noble prince was there, very anxious to reach France and land, so that he could help to recover his territory. But I was told that they were nine weeks at sea, and never got a fair wind; so they had to return, which made the king, prince and knights very downcast.

*How the prince complained of his great illness and asked his people to pray for him.* (1376)

Now I have told you the whole story of the prince's life; forgive me if I have passed over matters lightly, but a book as big as the romances of king Arthur, Alexander or Charlemagne could have been written about it, simply to record his deeds, prowess, largesse and wisdom, and to tell how he was always wise, loyal, catholic, and eager for the common good. He died nobly, acknowledging God as his Creator, and saying to his household: 'Lords, look at me, for God's sake; you see that we are not lords here. Everyone must go this way, and no-one can turn aside. I beg you in all humility to pray for me.'

*How the prince had the doors opened and his men brought in and thanked them
for their service, commending his young son to their care; and they wept
tenderly.*

Then he had the doors opened and all his men summoned who had
been his servants and had willingly served him. 'Lords,' he said,
'by my faith, you have served me loyally; I cannot reward you
properly myself, but God will do so in heaven.' Each wept heartfelt
tears, earls, barons and knights. He said in a loud voice: 'I commend
my son to you, who is young and small, and ask you to serve him
as you have served me.'

*How the prince called for his father the king and his brother the duke of
Lancaster and commended his wife and son to them, asking them to comfort
and look after them; and they promised to do so, with much sorrow.*

Then he called for his father, the king and his brother, the duke of
Lancaster; he commended his wife and son, whom he loved greatly,
to them, and begged them to help them. They swore on the Bible
to do so, and promised to comfort his children and uphold their
rights: all the princes and barons did this. The prince thanked them
a thousand times; but such grief was never seen as there was at his
death. The lovely princess felt such grief that her heart almost
burst. There was such a clamour of sighing, weeping, crying and
grieving that anyone alive would have felt pity at it.

*Of the noble and devout repentance of the prince, and of the date and place
of his death; here ends the book which Chandos Herald made.*

He made such a noble repentance that God will have mercy on his
soul; for he prayed to God to pardon all the misdeeds which he had
committed in this mortal world. And then the prince passed from
this world and died, on Trinity Sunday, 1376, at London; he had
always kept that feastday when he was alive. Now let us pray to
God, who died for us on the Cross, and He will forgive his soul
and grant him the glory of paradise. So ends the story of the noble
prince Edward, which the Herald Chandos told, and which he was
glad to write down.